ONLINE INVESTING the SmartWay

ONLINE INVESTING

THE SMART WAY

STEPHEN LITTAUER

DEARBORN™
A **Kaplan Professional** Company

Associate Publisher: Cynthia Zigmund
Managing Editor: Jack Kiburz
Project Editor: Trey Thoelcke
Interior Design: Lucy Jenkins
Cover Design: The Publishing Services Group
Typesetting: Elizabeth Pitts

Published by Dearborn
A Kaplan Professional Company

99 00 01 10 9 8 7 6 5 4 3 2 1

Library of Congress Cataloging-in-Publication Data

Littauer, Stephen L.
    Online investing the smart way / Stephen Littauer.
        p.   cm.
    Includes index.
    ISBN 0-7931-3424-2 (pbk.)
        1. Investments—Computer network resources.   I. Title.
    HG4515.95.L58   1999
    025.06'3326—dc21   99-29569
                                                    CIP

Dearborn books are available at special quantity discounts to use as premiums and sales promotions, or for use in corporate training programs. For more information, please call the Special Sales Manager at 800-621-9621, ext. 4514, or write to Dearborn Financial Publishing, Inc., 155 North Wacker Drive, Chicago, IL 60606-1719.

For Susan

I love our time together

OTHER BOOKS BY STEPHEN LITTAUER

Financial Independence the Smart Way

How to Invest the Smart Way

How to Buy Mutual Funds the Smart Way

How to Buy Stocks the Smart Way

C O N T E N T S

PART THREE

PART FOUR

PART FIVE

PREFACE

The boom in online trading has let ordinary investors cut out brokers as middlemen or at least reduce their role. Started only about five years ago, online investing has caused a dramatic shift in how the securities business is being conducted. Millions of people let their fingers do their investing, lured by the speed, convenience, and average $15 commissions of securities trading on the World Wide Web (Web). Increasingly, many investors never speak to a broker. They are part of a financial revolution.

E-investing, short for electronic investing, has evolved along with the Web. The emergence of discount brokers and the popularity of the Internet as a credible and seemingly bottomless source of investment information have given rise to do-it-yourself investing. The potential cost savings and practicality of the Web has easily led to the medium's transition from a research tool to a transaction tool for online investors.

According to the Securities Industry Association (www.sia.com), in 1997 more than 80 online brokerage firms held 5.3 million accounts worth an estimated $233 billion. This was up from 18 online firms with 1.5 million accounts with $111 billion in assets in 1996. By 1999 it was estimated that 30 percent of all stock trading was being done online through more than 100 firms. Forrester Research (www.forrester.com) predicted that computerized investing accounts will jump to 14.4 million in 2002, with assets managed online growing to $688 billion.

A steady stream of new technology continues to become available to investors. For instance, when a stock investor in Chatham, New Jersey, goes to lunch during the middle of the trading day, he's armed with all the technology he needs to conduct wireless trades over the Internet. With a "smart" cellular phone that alerts him if his stocks hit a set price, he can trade stocks over the Internet without a personal computer or laptop. Now it can be done with Internet-enabled smart phones, PalmPilots, or two-way pagers. A certified public accountant in Corrales, New Mexico, is also part of a growing number of people who handle Wall Street accounts on their own over the Internet. In an e-mail exchange with the *Macon Telegraph,* he stated: "I use it because the conventional wisdom of relying on 'professionals' is the easiest and fastest way to lose money. I am willing to live with the consequences of my own selections, as any serious investor should be."

Online trading offers investors a fast, convenient, and secure way to place trades and check account information over the Internet. Here are some of the benefits of online trading. You can

- place orders around the clock to buy and sell stocks, options, bonds, and mutual funds;
- enjoy substantially reduced commissions for stock, bond, and option trades;
- specify your orders as market, limit, stop, all or none, fill or kill, stop limit, or stop limit all or none (these orders are described later on);
- check your order status and change or cancel stock, bond, or option orders;
- obtain real-time or delayed quotes;
- view your brokerage account balances, holdings, and history; and
- communicate with your online firm through a secure messaging system.

It is important to remember that online investing is simply a tool that can help you invest more efficiently and effectively. Section I of *Online Investing the Smart Way* will help you get started online, learn where to find the best Internet sites, learn how to choose an online broker, and learn how to find investment opportunities in addition to other online opportunities and risks. But no investment tool can take the place of sound investment practices and strategies. Much of the information in later sections is designed to help you achieve investment success. You will learn how to develop your own long-term investment program, how to prepare a personal financial planning program on your computer, and how to invest wisely in stocks, bonds, and mutual funds.

You also will want to avoid the seven mistakes that can lead to investment disappointment. In-depth information about each of these problem areas is provided throughout the book:

1. *Unrealistic expectations for future investment returns.* Despite the market's strong performance since 1992, it is probable that average annual total returns on stocks, bonds, and cash invest-

ments will return to their long-term averages of 11 percent, 6 percent, and 4 percent, respectively.

2. *Allocating your assets based on past performance.* Although stocks have had spectacular returns in recent years, particularly large capitalization (large cap) stocks and those in certain favored sectors, it would be foolish to let those returns dictate how much of your portfolio you invest in stocks.

3. *Blindly following advice from personal finance gurus.* Be skeptical about what you read and hear. The boom in mutual funds and securities markets has helped fuel the growth of personal finance magazines, books, Web sites, and talk shows. When considering the torrent of advice and news tips, ask yourself: Who are the people giving the advice, and what are their qualifications?

4. *Failing to compare a mutual fund or a security with its peer group or a market index* [such as the Standard and Poor's 500-stock index (S&P 500)]. Comparing a fund or security with a peer group or market index is called *benchmarking* and is the best way to get a true measure of performance.

5. *Ignoring the impact of taxes and costs on long-term returns.* Remember, it's what you keep after taxes and costs that matters. When returns are very high, costs may seem almost trivial. But their impact becomes much more apparent during periods of normal returns.

6. *Being unprepared for market volatility.* Market downturns are inevitable, so be sure to factor them into your financial plans. Many investors are not prepared to ride out the sudden, and sometimes prolonged, drops that the market can dish out.

7. *Believing you can pick a winning stock or mutual fund in advance.* Picking a winning stock or fund in advance is not as easy as it looks. For instance, over the past ten years, only one in every ten general equity funds managed to outpace the S&P 500.

Most of us invest to provide ourselves with a financially secure future, but we have complex choices to make. Are you looking for current income, capital growth, future income, or some combination of these? Should your money be invested in stocks, bonds, mutual funds, or money market instruments? Successful long-term investing depends on sensible portfolio planning. This book is dedicated to helping you invest the smart way online. You will find commonsense principles of intelligent investing plus information that is essential to building your investment portfolio on a firm foundation.

The World of Online Investing

CHAPTER 1

Getting Started

Perhaps you've been buying stocks through a large, full-service brokerage firm but have not been particularly happy with the advice you've been getting. Now your broker has left the firm and no one has followed up with you. You are stuck with investments you don't know whether to hold or sell. Or perhaps you feel pressured by a broker who may be more interested in earning commissions than in growing your capital. Whatever the reason, you believe now may be the time to take control of your own investment transactions.

Millions of individual investors have taken the first step and opened an account with an online broker. One such investor told a reporter, "I've always been into computers, and the ability to do my own thing and not have to interact with a broker appealed to me." In the six years he has been trading electronically, he has used three different brokerage firms, switching whenever lower prices, greater convenience, or extra services enticed him. Right now he is using Vanguard Brokerage Services (www.vanguard.com), which charges a flat $20.00 commission on stock trades of up to 1,000 shares, 2¢ per share on trades of more than 1,000 shares, and lets him invest in all Vanguard mutual funds and about 800 non-Vanguard mutual funds without paying a transaction fee. Other investors, who do a high volume of trading, may deal through Datek (www.datek.com), a no-frills broker that charges a flat $9.99 commission on trades up to 5,000 shares.

These investors are part of a new breed who are seeking control, convenience, and cost savings. They tend to be independent and don't need hand-holding, or even contact with a human voice, and they're finding a home on the Internet. They like being able to check their account balances in the morning, and every few minutes during the day they can see the gain or loss in their portfolio or in particular stocks.

Some online investors caution that the technology also has some possible drawbacks. First, investors tend to trade more shares online than through full-commission brokerage firms or discount brokerage firms, according to online brokerage company E*TRADE Group (www.etrade.com). Online trading can also tempt investors into making less-disciplined decisions. Second, online discussion groups can pose another set of challenges. These groups may contain many incorrect or even fraudulent tips. Some online investors defend discussion groups as another means of participating directly online.

In early 1999 more than 5 million customers had online brokerage accounts, according to Forrester Research (www.forrester.com). That number will swell to more than 10 million by the end of 2000, Forrester estimates. According to the American Association of Individual Investors (www.aaii.com), more than 100 companies offer Internet trading, and more are logging on all the time with ever lower prices. One, Empire Financial Group (www.lowfees.com), even offers free trades if you buy or sell at least 1,000 shares of Nasdaq-traded stock priced at $5 or more a share (on market orders only). Among the companies currently online, 20 or so are considered major players based on price, service, or overall reputation.

Some full-service brokers have sites on the World Wide Web (the Web) and offer information online. But many have shied away from offering customers the ability to execute trades electronically because they're reluctant to undercut their commission business. According to Doug Alexander, president of Reality Online (www.realityonline. com), the full-service side of the business still accounts for 85 percent of brokers' commissions. He believes that in the end a large percentage of the population is going to want a human at the other end of the line.

Ready to Get Started?

If you are prepared to go it alone, you will find an increasingly friendly environment online. Many Web sites offer demonstrations of how to set up an account or execute a trade, but some sites require you to register even if you're just browsing, which can slow you down.

Commission schedules are clearly displayed. Understand, however, that the lowest fees generally apply to stock trades. Not all brokers trade mutual funds, and those that do may charge a different commission. You also may pay more to trade bonds or options, or to enter a limit order to buy or sell a security at a specific price. For instance, Ameritrade Holding Corporation (www.ameritrade.com) charges a flat commission of $8 on market orders for stock. There is an additional $5 charge for stop and limit orders. Low commissions are a boon to frequent traders, but small investors may be disappointed. Online brokers often have large minimum-balance requirements. One broker, which charges a flat $12 commission, requires a balance of $10,000.

You can access online brokers through commercial services such as America Online, CompuServe, and Prodigy, but you generally will find the lowest commissions on the Internet. For example, if you use Quick & Reilly through America Online, you will pay the standard commission less 10 percent, which would be $73.35 for 500 shares of an $18 stock. That compares with a flat fee of $14.95 for all market orders, and $19.95 for all limit orders up to 5,000 shares on the Internet. For the fastest and best service, you need a powerful and secure Web browser, such as Netscape Navigator or Microsoft Internet Explorer; some sites are not accessible with anything less.

If you are a frequent trader, commissions can be critical in choosing a broker. Of course, the lower the commission, the less you can expect in the way of research assistance. Some services have links to other Web sites that provide research reports, charts, earnings estimates, and analysts' advice. You may wish to supplement your broker's resources on your own. The Money & Investing ActiveX Portfolio is an alternative to the standard portfolio on the Excite site (www.excite. com). With it you can view and track your investments. Prices and portfolio values are updated either on demand or on a scheduled basis.

Not every online broker's service is bare bones, however; a number of them offer personalized bells and whistles. For example, E*TRADE customers can get continuously updated quotes on the prices of stocks they follow even after they've left the E*TRADE site. DLJdirect, Inc. (www.dljdirect.com) allows customers to create a personalized stock ticker and also offers a free search engine that helps investors select mutual funds using criteria such as fund objective and manager's tenure. With proprietary software, Accutrade (www.accutrade.com) will let you trade a group of stocks—a feature the company likens to managing your own mutual fund.

Just about all the online brokers offer free 15-minute-delayed quotes. Some, like Datek and Net Investor (www.netinvestor.com), offer free real-time quotes.

Customer Service

Customer service varies dramatically among online brokers. DLJdirect, for instance, has registered representatives available 365 days a year to answer customers' questions. If you place a trade with Charles Schwab (www.schwab.com) that is unusual for your account, the computer will flag it and a broker will call you. At Net Investor (www.netinvestor.com) an order is personally scanned. On the other hand, E*TRADE and Ameritrade are highly automated, so you are basically on your own. Most online brokers will e-mail trade confirmations, and nearly all firms send confirmations by regular mail. A few offer a personal touch and will confirm your trade by phone.

Safety

Security is the biggest concern for many investors who are considering online trading. For starters, there is the fear that somebody will be able to interrupt your trade, change it in some way, or keep you from completing your transaction. Although brokers can't guarantee such things won't happen, they are working together to set up safety standards and systems equipped with a full panoply of online safety measures, including secure browsers. According to Don Montanaro of Quick & Reilly, all brokers are using the same cutting-edge technology. Just as you will never see American Airlines advertise that it has fewer crashes than United, you won't see one broker advertise that it has better online security than another.

Many investors also worry that a hacker will crack the system and see what they are trading. Again, online brokers can't guarantee that won't happen. But they say such an invasion of privacy also could occur if you use a traditional broker with whom your telephone conversations might be overheard or your account statements photocopied. When your statements are mailed over the Internet, they have greater safety because they are encrypted.

There is also the fear that someone will be able to tap into your account and transfer your retirement funds to an offshore bank account. But few firms permit money to be withdrawn over the Internet—a point you might want to check with your broker if you are concerned about security.

Finally, there is a perception that online brokers aren't as solid as traditional brokers. Even though they operate in cyberspace without the benefit of bricks and mortar, online brokers are subject to the same regulations and capital requirements as other brokers. The Securities Investor Protection Corporation (SIPC) insures securities accounts against a firm's failure for $500,000 per customer, and most brokers pay for additional coverage through private insurers.

IN A NUTSHELL

New state-of-the-art systems assure you of private, secure access to your online account. In addition, you can access your account 24 hours a day, 7 days a week. Of course, trades are executed during normal market hours. Once a trade is placed, you may choose the method of confirmation you prefer: telephone, e-mail, or fax. You also can get quotes and check your positions and balances with just a click of your mouse.

The Best Internet Sites for Investors

The best investment Web sites provide more information more quickly and in a better-organized fashion than could be imagined just a few years ago. The Internet provides individuals with what once was available only on Wall Street trading desks. In fact, it now offers more. You can stick with the free sites or subscribe to others for a monthly fee. Here are some of the best, listed in order of my preference.

Microsoft MoneyCentral

In the vanguard is Microsoft MoneyCentral (moneycentral.com). Like so many other Microsoft offerings, it was no overnight success. It took a few versions to arrive at its present level of competence. The site offers free real-time quotes, a graphical overview of your portfolio, and technical charting tools. Its interface refinements make the site fast and easy to navigate. MoneyCentral's high quality stems from a number of things: It provides timely news and analysis with *Wall Street Journal* updates five times a day plus news and insight generated by editorial staff members and outside contributors. You can create charts and pick up Securities and Exchange Commission (SEC) filings, and access other current data and news articles.

Microsoft has put together a carefully selected amalgam of the features and information a large body of individual investors might need. For instance, Microsoft's free Research Wizard effectively uses a multiscreen scheme to walk new investors through the process of researching a security. Each screen in the sequence uses learning aids like tables, links, and comparative tools—all focused on the particular security you are researching.

Subscriptions cost $9.95 per month, with a free 30-day trial offer. Paid features include stock and fund screeners (including an investment matcher that finds similar securities based on criteria such as market capitalization), an inside view of the strategies of six professional investment advisers, insider trading, and analyst recommendations in addition to alerts triggered by significant events that may affect your investments.

Note that features similar to some of those offered by Microsoft are available free elsewhere, but this site offers a carefully crafted assembly of features and usability.

CBS MarketWatch

CBS MarketWatch (marketwatch.com) offers a good portfolio tracker, a reasonably thorough stock screener, a charting utility with tools for technical analysis, and direct links to data from companies such as Hoover's and Zacks Investment Research. Its *Getting Personal* section offers helpful reading if you are looking for market insight and guidance, and industry names like Thom Calandra and Paul Farrell offer their takes on current financial events. The standard data are there in abundance, retrievable individually or in quantified groupings— earnings surprises, initial public offerings, and so on.

Like MoneyCentral, CBS MarketWatch delivers a lot of the same tools offered on other investment sites. But its strengths lie in reporting and analyzing breaking news and its ability to select a set of features that will likely appeal to many individual investors in a clear, lively interface. All are free and come with tools for both beginners (most notably an impressive investing primer) and experienced investors.

Yahoo! Finance

Yahoo! Finance (quote.yahoo.com) is a very successful model for competing Web sites (a lot of sites look like Yahoo), but Yahoo! Finance sticks to its straightforward, fast—though not so interesting— front page. Nobody, however, has a better design, at least in terms of financial information. This site doesn't really have an editorial voice of its own but draws on some of the best in the industry for content, from places like TheStreet.com (www.thestreet.com) and The Motley Fool (www.fool.com). It also offers a lot of market data and financial news (U.S. and international) so that you can probably find what you need there. Market news is highlighted at the bottom of the page, and links—the cornerstone of Yahoo's existence—are abundant.

Yahoo has a surprisingly generous set of tools that includes a stock screener, message boards and a stock chat area, a pager that can be triggered by your own specific stock price limits, and a Java portfolio. Yahoo's integration makes it easy once you get going. Set up a basic portfolio, for example, and one page displays quotes and charts, current news, and links to research and related user messages. Many elements of the site's layout are easily modified, and everything is free.

CNNfn

The opening page of CNNfn doesn't reveal much about the depth of this site. Every link on the home page (cnnfn.com) leads to another set of links within; sometimes there is another and then another. The site takes a very straightforward linear approach and is not at all difficult to use. What CNNfn lacks in its interface design is more than made up for in sheer volume of news and data, timeliness, and analysis.

CNNfn has a partnership with Quicken.com (www.quicken. com)—with extra investment tools the partnership brings. Quicken. com on fn (cnnfn.com/quickenonfn), a separate section of the site, weaves together screens and links from both Quicken.com and CNNfn to produce a powerful package of tools, breaking news, and other data and analysis. Quicken's contributions to the site include a customizable portfolio tracker, stock screener and picks, an interactive retirement planner, and the *Lipper Mutual Fund Report*. The site is completely free of charge, and its simplicity makes navigation speedy despite its depth.

Quicken.com

In terms of data and analysis, commentary, and tools and interactivity, Quicken.com is among the best of the investment sites (www.quicken. com). And everything is free. Like MoneyCentral, this is a full-service personal finance site that incorporates such related issues as banking, mortgages, and insurance. But its investment features are strong on their own. The portfolio tracker's columns are customizable: You can choose from 4 predefined column sets (valuation, equity fundamentals, holdings summary, and price performance) or build your own from 12 choices. You also can set alerts that are triggered by events like announcements of stock splits.

Quicken.com also draws on the expertise of other sites. Market data come from Briefing.com (www.briefing.com) and Standard & Poor's, and commentary comes from TheStreet.com as well as from CBS MarketWatch reporters. A stock screener and mutual fund finder are joined by a stock evaluator that lets you compare two or more stocks using various ratios and fundamental measures like price/sales and earnings per share.

Morningstar.Net

To many investors, Morningstar (www.morningstar.net) may be synonymous with mutual funds, but its Web site is a mecca for individual investors, whether they are into funds or individual stocks. The opening page resembles a slick magazine, with all of the site's contents clearly identified up front. Top news and features are displayed in two of the three columns, and the third holds links to some of the site's best tools, such as the stock and fund selectors. Basic versions of both are free, but more advanced features are limited to subscribers at $9.95 per month.

Quicktake reports are available from opening page links. Enter a security symbol and Morningstar.Net pops open a tabbed file folder graphic with six data categories, including financials, growth trends, price/ownership, and valuation. Much of the data comes free, but some things, like earnings trends and return on equity analysis, are for subscribers only.

The Morningstar site is divided into several sections: Learn (guidance for novices); Plan (assistance to help you develop your own); Research (investment data and analysis); Invest (hands-on trading information and advice); Monitor (more market updates and commentary, and portfolio tracking); and Socialize (topic-related and company-related message boards). Despite its depth, Morningstar.Net is a clean, fast site.

TheStreet.com

This is the place (www.thestreet.com) for informed, expert analysis of the investment scene before, during, and after the trading day. Head pundit Jack Cramer, backed by a talented staff and contributors like Herb Greenberg, gives this site credibility and a unique blend of voices. Targeted, timely market updates, voluminous feature stories about companies in the news, and an entire section devoted to articles and columns about mutual funds (usually several daily) give you more analysis and opinion than you probably have time to read. The site's investor tool kit includes standard investing tools like a portfolio tracker, stock/fund charting, and access to Thomson reports. Free section: daily stories about the markets plus tools are clearly marked. Access to the site costs $6.95 a month. For $9.95 you also get twice-a-day e-mail bulletins.

ZD Interactive Investor

The opening page (www.zdii.com) of this site emphasizes breaking news. Links to the latest news stories and snapshots of current market activity (winners, losers, global view, and a brief view of the U.S. markets) dominate the page. Enter a symbol in the Quote field and ZDII returns a page incorporating a delayed price, with links to a full quote, comparative charts, related news and SEC filings, a company profile, key financial figures, and names of competitors. This is a nice, speedy tool.

Stockpoint

Stockpoint's site (www.stockpoint.com) has been carefully conceived and executed. It is clean, simple, understandable, and fast. Eric Tyson, author of *Investing for Dummies,* is a regular contributor. Briefing.com, whose insightful analysis appears on other Web sites, also contributes editorial material here. News briefs and in-depth stories come from such sources as Comtex, UPI, and Businesswire. The market data screens capture all of the key numbers from the day. Securities quotes are supported by a variety of supplemental material such as analysts' ratings and an interactive chart feature that lets you apply technical indicators, compare indexes and securities, and specify chart types and dates.

The Motley Fool

The Motley Fool (www.fool.com) has two real strengths: its sense of community and its commonsense, folksy approach. *The Fool's School* teaches the 13 steps to investing, according to the site's founders. This is one of the best sites for beginners because of its friendly tone and understandable verbiage. Experienced investors will find a lot here too, and everything is free. But don't look for reams and reams of data from the outside. That is not the Fool's focus. Research tools are adequate for the casual investor. Portfolios link to customizable charts, news, estimates, and other data plus an entire section devoted to interesting stock ideas.

The message boards of this site are some of the liveliest you will find anywhere. There are informative articles on just about any personal finance subject imaginable, with lots of input from experts and other contributors. It's not the best site for breaking news and analysis, though it does offer some of both. Go on the site for an ongoing discussion of news and stocks.

Briefing.com

This site (www.briefing.com) is an excellent research and analysis tool for the very serious investor. Though it offers some free features, its premium services cost either $6.96 or $25.00 per month, depending on the package you select. The site's real strength is its continuous analysis of the market throughout the trading day and its wrapups and other commentary outside market hours. The free introductory package offers quotes, charting, and commentary. For $6.95 you get more focused information more often, such as analyses of technology stocks and upgrades and downgrades. The pricier package adds running analyses of the credit and currency markets, similar to services aimed at bond-trading desks and costing hundreds of dollars a month.

IN A *N*UTSHELL

You can access more quick, concise, objective information from your computer than could be imagined just a few years ago. Whether you have just started investing or are a seasoned professional, the Internet provides you with what was once available only on Wall Street trading desks. In fact, it now offers more. You can stick with the free sites or subscribe to others for a monthly fee.

The Best Online Brokers—and How to Choose One

You would like to know which online trading firm has the best, most reliable service. Do you mean today? At 3 PM? Or maybe a month from now on that day when the market goes into a nosedive and you must make a trade. Things change very quickly in the online world. With the popularity of Web-based trading growing so fast and the technology so new, even the best-run trading system can be overwhelmed in periods of peak demand or fall prey to some unavoidable glitch.

In early 1999, Charles Schwab Corporation (www.schwab.com) dominated the booming business of trading stocks online. Its giant computing center in Phoenix handled almost one-third of all Internet trading—meaning that 1 in 20 stock trades in America passed through the Schwab system. According to Gomez Advisors (www.gomez.com), an Internet consultancy that rates online trading firms, Schwab's Web service ranks number 8 out of 20, in part because its $29.95 fee for each trade is at the top end of an industry in which $8.00 trades are no longer unusual. But at that time, Schwab was perhaps the only online broker to have grown out of its capacity problems, being able to handle 88,000 online customers at one time. E*TRADE, by contrast, had three days within a week when its trading system crashed, and Ameritrade also had a costly shutdown.

Serious individual investors should approach online trading and selection of a broker the same way they would a trip to the wilderness: Be ready for anything.

Seven Cautionary Tips to Bear in Mind

1. No way are you able to predict when the next record volume day will be or who will have capacity problems. No one has unlimited capacity. So consider opening a second account with a different online brokerage. If your primary account is with a popular firm such as Charles Schwab, consider going with a smaller, less heavily trafficked brokerage.
2. It's hard to turn down the cheapest trading rates, but price means nothing if you can't trade on busy days. If you want to avoid the hassle of having more than one trading account, then choose a firm with multiple trading channels—Internet, proprietary software, telephone, and in person. That way, if one service goes down, you have an alternative.
3. On a day with heavy trading volume, it is nearly impossible to determine if a slowdown is your problem, the brokerage firm's problem, or a problem with the Internet. Make sure your Internet service provider (ISP) performs well in periods of heavy usage. You may want to open a second Internet access account with a different ISP. That way, you have an emergency account in place if one connection isn't working. If you are serious about trading online, you should also make sure your computer is up to the job—it's no secret that the Internet is more efficient on computers packing one of the newer, faster chips. With equipment prices dropping continuously, investing in an upgrade may be worth your while.
4. If you aren't an investor who watches the market during the day and trades with price movements, place your orders at night or very early in the morning when fewer people are online. You can place an order to buy or sell at a set price that you specify, called a limit order. But watch out: If you see the market going one way and want to cancel your limit order, you may not be able to get back in before the order is executed.
5. During high-volume days, brace yourself for the fact that things might be rough and you may just have to wait. Even the biggest firms have had execution troubles (this can happen too with investors who trade the old-fashioned way on the phone or in person with a broker). Also try to be somewhat flexible with your price. If you see one price flash on your screen, don't always expect to get it. In a fast-moving market, prices change quickly and the tape you're watching may be behind.

6. If you don't get any response to your ongoing complaints about service and execution, you can always turn to the National Association of Securities Dealers (NASD). You can find out how to file a complaint at the NASD Web site (www.nasd.com). The complaint form is available to you right there online.
7. Last, if your livelihood depends on your daily trading, trading exclusively via the Web may not be best for you. Some day traders have given up trying to get through to their Web-based brokerage accounts. Instead, they do their business in a local day trading shop, renting a dedicated trading terminal.

Selecting an Online Broker

Power is what trading stocks in cyberspace is all about. Online trading is based on the immediate execution of orders, buying and selling with the touch of a key, and the ability to check your portfolio at any time, day or night. Now, e-brokers are luring even the most casual investors with low commissions, a wealth of easily accessible research, and up-to-the-minute stock prices.

But the features that make online trading so appealing to investors are, surprisingly, not offered by all online brokers. Traders constantly complain about being unable to log on to their accounts or complete trades instantly, as many of the brokerages promise. These problems, of course, worsen on days with heavy market activity.

One of the best of the online brokers is a relative newcomer: Web Street Securities. This firm combines low commissions and fees with around-the-clock service and speedy technical support. Web Street also provides free real-time quotes and online account information that is immediately updated. But Web Street falls short on free research, lacking links to analysts' recommendations and mutual fund data. Other top-rated firms include Datek Online and Discover Brokerage Direct. Both offer low commissions and free real-time quotes but fall short in online investment products. Although American Express gets high marks for account information, research, and technical support, you'll pay high fees and additional charges for real-time quotes: Figure 3.1 lists some of the top online firms with their Web addresses and charges per trade in early 1999.

FIGURE 3.1 / SOME TOP ONLINE BROKERAGE FIRMS

The basic commission refers to the lowest rates for stock trades made over the Internet. Aside from no-transaction-fee mutual funds, a different commission structure may apply to fund trades. Commissions are generally higher for trading bonds, Treasury securities, or options; and most brokers charge extra for stock certificates and wire transfers. Contact them for current information.

Accutrade
www.accutrade.com
800-494-8939

Basic commission: $29.95 for Internet stock trades up to 1,000 shares.

American Express
www.americanexpress.com/direct
800-658-4667

Basic commission: $24.95 for Internet stock trades up to 4,000 shares.

Ameritrade
www.ameritrade.com
800-326-7507

Basic commission: $8.00 for any number of Internet market order trades.

Datek Online
www.datek.com
888-463-2835

Basic commission: $9.99 for Internet stock trades up to 5,000 shares.

Discover Brokerage
www.discoverbrokerage.com
800-688-3462

Basic commission: $14.95 for market order Internet stock trades up to 5,000 shares.

DLJ Direct
www.dljdirect.com
800-825-5723

Basic commission: $20.00 for Internet stock trades up to 1,000 shares, then 2¢ for each share thereafter.

Empire Financial Group, Inc.
www.lowfees.com
800-900-8101

Basic commission: $6.95 for market order Internet trades on listed stocks up to 5,000 shares. No commission for Nasdaq market orders of 1,000 shares or more for stocks priced at $5.00 or more.

E*TRADE
www.etrade.com
800-786-2575

Basic commission: $14.95 for Internet trades on listed stocks up to 5,000 shares.

Fidelity
www.fidelity.com
800-544-8666

Basic commission: $19.95 up to 1,000 shares.

Lombard
www.lombard.com
800-566-2273

Basic commission: $14.95 for market order Internet trades on listed stocks up to 5,000 shares.

National Discount Brokers
www.ndb.com
800-888-3999

Basic commission: $14.75 for market order Internet trades up to 5,000 shares.

FIGURE 3.1 / SOME TOP ONLINE BROKERAGE FIRMS (CONTINUED)

Net Investor
www.netinvestor.com
800-638-4250

Basic commission: $19.95 plus 1¢ per share for Internet stock trades.

Quick & Reilly
www.quickwaynet.com
800-672-7220

Basic commission: $14.95 for market orders on Internet equity trades.

Charles Schwab
www.schwab.com
800-435-4000

Basic commission: $29.95 for equity trades on the Internet up to 1,000 shares.

Suretrade
www.suretrade.com
401-642-6900

Basic commission: $7.95 for Internet market order trades of less than 5,000 shares.

Vanguard Brokerage Services
www.vanguard.com
800-992-8327

Basic commission: $20.00 or 2¢ per share, whichever is greater, for Internet market order or limit order trades.

Wall Street Access
www.wsaccess.com
888-925-5782

Basic commission: $25.00 on Internet equity trades up to 5,000 shares.

Waterhouse Securities
www.waterhouse.com
800-934-4134

Basic commission: $12.00 on Internet equity trades up to 5,000 shares.

A. B. Watley
www.abwatley.com
888-229-2853

Basic commission: $9.95 on Internet equity trades up to 5,000 shares.

Web Street Securities
www.webstreetsecurities.com
800-932-0438

Basic commission: $14.95 on any Internet trade of listed stocks, any size. No commission on Nasdaq stock trades of 1,000 shares or more.

Jack White
www.jackwhiteco.com
800-753-1700

Basic commission: $25.00 per Internet equity trade up to 1,250 shares.

Wit Capital
www.witcapital.com
888-494-8227

Basic commission: $14.95 for Internet trades of listed stocks up to 1,000 shares.

Criteria to Consider in Online Brokers

Some of the criteria you will want to consider in choosing an online broker are discussed below. Because of the complex and ever changing mix of services brokers provide, use the Web addresses listed in Figure 3.1 to access those firms that interest you and get their current offerings.

Commissions

Online investing has reduced the cost of investing considerably. Suretrade has rapidly built a customer base, charging only $7.95 a trade. Suretrade's commissions are one-half as expensive as those of the average online broker. Ameritrade follows at $8.00 per trade and, unlike most of its competitors, does not charge extra for large orders. (Most firms tack on an additional charge per share for trades over 1,000 or 5,000 shares). At firms such as Accutrade and Charles Schwab, investors pay rates of more than three times the cheapest. Web Street, on the other hand, offers commission-free trades for Nasdaq orders of more than 1,000 shares (on shares that are more than $2).

Real-Time Quotes

Real-time quotes are what online trading is supposed to be all about. Surprisingly, although delayed quotes seem as archaic as checking stock prices in a newspaper, not all online brokerages offer free real-time quotes. But more are doing so. Some firms offer a minimum of 100 free real-time quotes, and a few give customers unlimited quotes. Others offer too few free real-time quotes (in most cases just one) to be of use to an active trader and charge as much as $30 for unlimited quotes.

Account Information

Logging on to your account in the middle of the day—or even at the market close—may bring up information that is nearly a day old. And although many brokerages automatically update trades on your online account summary, few keep your portfolio balance updated in real time. But a few firms do, including Web Street, Datek, and Discover Brokerage Direct, as well as updating prices of individual securities in portfolios in real time. Others, such as American Express,

Ameritrade, Schwab, and National Discount Brokerage, come close, updating prices of securities in portfolios every 15 to 20 minutes.

Technical Support

A wide range of online broker technical support is available to investors. Although all firms offer technical support via e-mail, few guarantee you will receive a response the same day. Requesting support by telephone can be time consuming and frustrating. For instance, at Ameritrade and E*TRADE I have had a consistently long wait, but nothing topped the agonizingly long wait at Suretrade. The least amount of time on the phone is likely to be spent with Web Street and Fidelity; both companies offer around-the-clock assistance seven days a week.

Fees

Check out your broker's fees for such items as wiring money, electronically transferring money, individual retirement accounts (IRAs), bounced checks, and other account charges. They can add up quickly. Sometimes you will find that the lower the commission an online broker charges, the higher and more numerous are the fees. For instance, although you will be paying higher commissions at Charles Schwab than at most other firms, its fees are among the lowest. The extras will add up at American Express, especially if you ever need to wire or electronically transfer money—you'll pay $50 for that service. American Express also ranks among the highest in margin rates an investor has to pay, nearly three percentage points higher than the rate charged by Datek. Following are examples of fees charged by Ameritrade.

Certificate delivery	$15
Special registration	15
Real-time quotes	20 (per month)
Funds wired out	15
Legal item	25
Returned check	25
Stop payments	25
Transfer out of account	25
Certain IRA transactions	25

Products

Online firms have made notable progress in offering a variety of investment products without requiring investors to even pick up the telephone. Although you may never be able to buy commodities, futures, or variable annuities on the Net, brokerages are increasingly expanding their online offerings that now include American depositary receipts (ADRs), high-yield bonds, and even initial public offerings (IPOs). Some firms offer all of these in addition to stocks (listed, over-the-counter, and penny), mutual funds, IRAs, Keogh plans, bonds, and options.

Research Links

Free data on stocks and mutual funds, company reports, and analyst recommendations are all available right at your fingertips. Quick & Reilly offers customers access to enough research to complement its wide product offerings. You will find data from such experts as Standard & Poor's Corporation and First Call on Schwab's site. Both Charles Schwab and Quick & Reilly offer historical data on price, volume, and dividends as well as analyst recommendations and reports— all at no charge. Most online brokers are increasing the amount of research available at their sites for you to use.

Opening an Online Account

Brokers who operate online generally give you the option of filling out an application they provide by mail or using the interactive application found at their Web site. If you use the Web site application, you must print the form from your computer, sign in the appropriate places, and mail the original copy to the broker. Other forms you may need for IRAs, trusts, partnerships, or other types of accounts may be found at the Web site, or you can request them by telephone.

IN A NUTSHELL

Approach online trading and selection of a broker the same way you would a trip to the wilderness: Be ready for anything. Trading stocks in cyberspace offers you immediate execution of orders, buying and selling with the touch of a key, and being able to check your portfolio at any time, day or night. Now, even the most casual investors have access to low commissions, a wealth of easily accessible research, and up-to-the-minute stock prices.

CHAPTER 4

Screening for Investment Opportunities

Thanks to new online software, you can tailor your stock portfolio like the pros. Internet stock-screening programs, which provide the same tools that professionals use, are available at several Web sites. The programs are fast and offer a wide array of information without the need for particular expertise. For the expert and novice alike, you can have an investing miracle delivered to your own computer screen. Ever since computers were harnessed to the task of choosing investments, portfolio managers have used screens to sift through mountains of stock market data to unearth the best shares.

It is not the breadth of information alone that makes stock screens so special. A sizable portion of their beauty lies in speed. Generally speaking, counting the amount of time it takes to log on, you will spend only five to ten minutes to input a set of orders and collect a list of stocks. That means it is now possible to tailor a portfolio to fit your needs, risk tolerance, and future plans in one sitting. Better yet, you need not have a degree in computer programming or have great investing expertise to get started. And consider the price of the advice; in many cases it's free!

What exactly is a stock screen? You may remember seeing movies depicting crusty old prospectors panning mountain streams in search of gold. They would dip into the river's silt, swirl the mud and water about a bit, skim the contents, and collect the shiniest rocks. A stock screen works much like the prospector's pan. Its software scoops up data on thousands of stocks that trade publicly on the New York Stock Exchange, American Stock Exchange, and the Nasdaq. Next, it sifts through the numbers according to requirements or criteria you plug in, discarding the companies that don't meet your goals. For example, if you are looking for corporations that are growing earnings at 20 percent or more a year but are trading at a price-earnings (PE) ratio (also known as the multiple) of 30 or less, a screen will ferret out a list of candidates for you to examine—a marked break with the past.

Not long ago, the average individual investor's stock-picking efforts were a hit-or-miss venture. Choosing a company you would invest in amounted to wading through mounds of annual reports, scanning an endless array of numbers, or just plain luck based on a tip from a friend. Spending extra money in trading commissions might get you a few recommendations from your broker.

If you have never used stock screens, don't worry. This chapter will get you started with some ideas and places to go online. Start with the screens themselves, which can be found at a number of sites on the Web. Here are two suggestions as you start off: Keep it simple and make sure it's free.

Screens on the Net come in two varieties: beginning and advanced. If you are just getting the knack of how stocks are valued and how the market works, the fact that the online sites provide hand-holding is good news. Be aware, however, that, at the very least, you need to know the basics.

A quick course includes learning about PEs; a PE is derived by dividing a stock's price by its profits (earnings per share). Investors use PEs to compare the value of one share with another. Then there are earnings growth rates, which amount to educated guesses about how quickly a company is growing profits annually. It's also good to have a grasp of dividends (profits a company regularly distributes to shareholders quarterly) and yields (a stock's dividend divided by its current share price). Beyond that, many screens delve into more detailed measures, including price-to-book ratios (a stock's share price divided by the value of its assets) or return on equity, a measure of how company management uses its cash resources from shareholders.

The Database

No matter how large or small, stock screens work with large pools of information, called a database. They include a library of company names and the one-letter to five-letter ticker symbols that investors use to identify stocks (INTC for Intel or GM for General Motors). Screens also are loaded with an enormous amount of company-specific facts and figures—earnings growth rates, for example, to point out how quickly the management of a company is expanding its sales and earnings. PEs indicate whether shares are cheap or expensive relative to the market or to a company's peers.

But a screen is only as good as the facts and figures it is accessing. Often stock screens tap into companies that poll industry analysts at the big Wall Street brokerage firms such as Merrill Lynch and Salomon Smith Barney. Firms like I/B/E/S, Zacks, and First Call, to name a few of the most reputable, then combine numbers, tabulate averages, and provide consensus figures, or averages, of what Wall Street projects for a company. A good screening program will serve up those kinds of numbers for your review.

Remember, too, that fresh data ensure your screen will be up to date, for things on Wall Street can change overnight. For instance, Byte Size Books.com might release news to the press that its new superstrategy for overtaking its Web competition in selling books via the Internet didn't make as much money during the last quarter as expected. Almost automatically, analysts will sharpen their pencils, rush headlong through their earlier analyses, and lower their estimates of revenues, earnings, and even the rate they feel Byte Size can grow its profits.

The market takes these sorts of assumptions seriously because they help determine how much a stock is worth now and in the future. Needless to say, the figures stockpiled by consensus estimate firms will probably dip as well. To provide the most accurate figures, a good screen will update its reservoir of numbers regularly. Figure 4.1 lists several free stock screen sites. All update daily and use solid sources for their data. Perhaps the simplest and most straightforward can be found on Quicken's site, where you can screen the entire market or go industry by industry, using a no-nonsense format.

MarketPlayer is by far the most comprehensive in its choice of different criteria but can be a bit daunting if you're just learning to screen. Some of the terms—for example, *forward PE* (a company's price-earnings ratio for the upcoming year)—may be a bit much for initial investors. You might want to go first to the simple screening heading in the left margin of the site or try your hand at a few of the model screens provided. Another solution: Click on the support heading in the left margin and send a query for assistance to MarketPlayer

---

FIGURE 4.1 / STOCK SCREEN SITES

TITLE	ADDRESS
Quicken	www.quicken.com/investments/stocks/search
Marketplayer	www.marketplayer.com
DailyStocks	www.dailystocks.com
Hoover's	www.stockscreener.com

---

via e-mail. A page in the MarketPlayer screening application is reproduced in Figure 4.2.

DailyStocks not only offers a choice of screens but also has links to a veritable diamond mine of company and stock information. Again, the terminology can get a bit heavy; as an entry point, try clicking at the heading Quick Pre-Screened. There you will find a number of preset screens to help you get up to speed. Finally, you might want to check in at Hoover's site.

Screening for Good Ideas and Picks

Where to start? One surefire method is to copy the moves the pros use. Money managers who are looking for companies that can grow earnings quickly often resort to a tried-and-true rule: Never pay for a stock whose PE is greater than its anticipated earnings growth rate. Translated into hard numbers, that means if IBM is predicted to grow earnings at about 20 percent a year, its shares look good at a PE of 20 or less but are not so tempting at a PE above 20.

You also can copy some of the many tricks of the trade that value managers—the market's bargain shoppers—like to use. One is to look for companies whose PEs are well below that of the market, as measured by an index like the Standard & Poor's 500 (S&P 500). If the S&P 500 on average has a PE of 20, that means shares in the range of 16 or lower might be attractive. Dividends are another yardstick for value investors. If a stock's yield (its dividend divided by its current price) is above that of the S&P 500 (in early 1999 at about 1.5 percent), value investors are looking at a possible bargain. Another bargain indicator is price-to-book value. A company trading at two to three times its book value or less—the worth of its concrete assets like factory

FIGURE 4.2 / MARKETPLAYER SCREENING APPLICATION

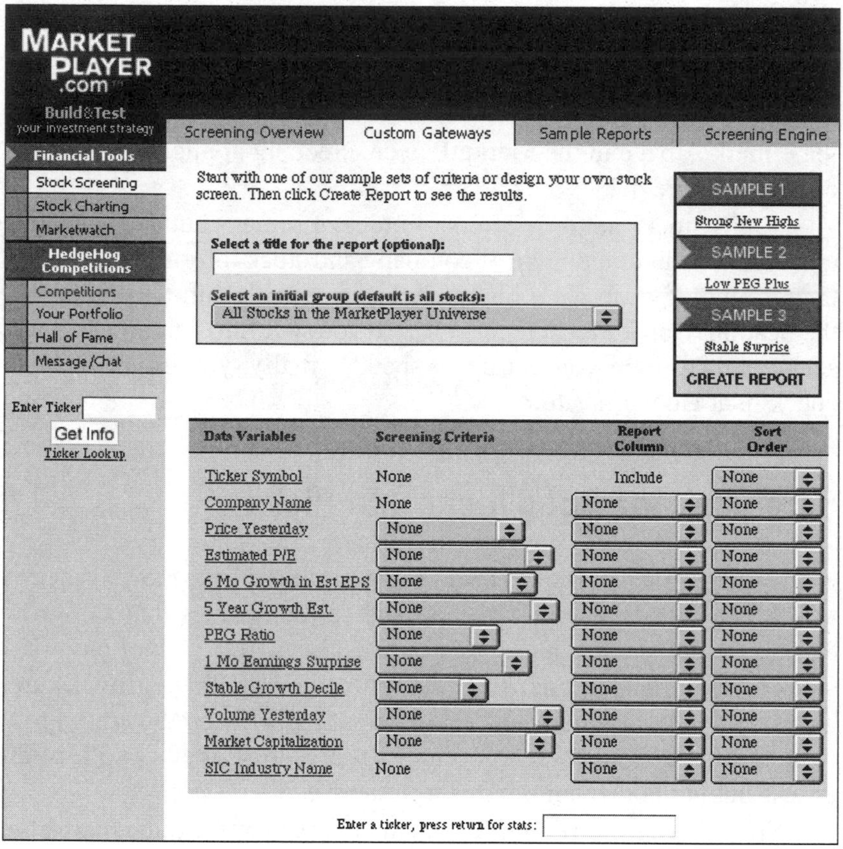

space and inventory—will get a considerable number of value investment pros interested in finding out more.

There are different criteria that both value and growth investors use. Debt-to-equity ratio, an indicator of just how much a company is in debt, is one. Many money managers will say that they never look twice at a company with debt as high as 40 percent of its equity.

It goes without saying that there are as many investment styles as there are managers. In many cases, it is possible to mix and match criteria depending on your preferences or even your whims.

Keep in mind other sources for ideas. Personal finance sections on many sites feature ideas from analysts and commentators. There you will find hints, tips, and techniques used by portfolio managers. Institutional and mutual fund managers explain their investment strategies. Mutual fund prospectuses and funds' online sites can offer a wealth of investment strategies as well. One thing you can do is dig up a few of a fund's holdings to quickly determine what biases may guide a manager in selecting stocks.

The Next Step

You have now screened and screened again. A few stocks have caught your fancy. You might be tempted to call it a day and be done. Don't. Once the screening is completed, your work has just begun. After you have narrowed the investing universe to workable dimensions, you still have to look a bit closer at companies and their respective industries. In financial terms, this is called a *bottom-up approach.*

Because you may not be in a position to sit down to lunch with management, you would do well to read in financial magazines about a company that interests you to see what is currently going on at headquarters. The reason: Company data, no matter where they come from, are fallible. Because chief executive officers don't always tell the whole story, the due diligence effort belongs to you.

Again you can turn to the Internet for further research. Sources include DailyStocks, which is crammed with links to financial publications and journals. The U.S. Securities and Exchange Commission (SEC) (www.sec.gov) is the government repository for company filings. Finally, you can call the investor relations department at any publicly owned company to receive an annual report and other financial data.

FIGURE 4.3 / MUTUAL FUND SCREENS

TITLE	ADDRESS
FundFocus	www.fundfocus.com
Morningstar	www.morningstar.net
SmartMoney	www.smartmoney.com

Put together the screening capabilities the pros use and good research to back it up, and you should be well on your way to becoming your own successful portfolio manager.

Mutual Fund Screens

The same screening power that places the entire stock market in your hands is also available for mutual funds. You can screen on any of dozens of factors. A number of excellent fund screen sites let you search their databases of more than 6,000 funds to zero in on the few funds that meet your needs. The sites cover a number of key questions; and a few sites are listed in Figure 4.3.

FundFocus tells you how long the fund manager has been running the fund, what the fund's average annual return is over a given number of years, and what the fund's expense ratio is. It also tells you each fund's investment objective, its performance relative to its peers, its load/fee structure, its relative risk, and its minimum investment amount. Fund-Focus is also an excellent launching spot, where you can work with a number of criteria and research the funds you choose after screening.

SmartMoney's site (shown in Figure 4.4) offers a large number of criteria choices under the categories of performance, grades, volatility, profile, expenses, and family. Once you have made your selections, click on the search button to see a sortable table of the funds that meet your standards. For an even more detailed view of how the best funds stack up against one another, click the Analyze First 15 Funds tab.

Morningstar's site presents a battery of simple screens for beginners to use, although the more advanced screens require a subscription to the service.

FIGURE 4.4 / SMARTMONEY MUTUAL FUND SCREENER

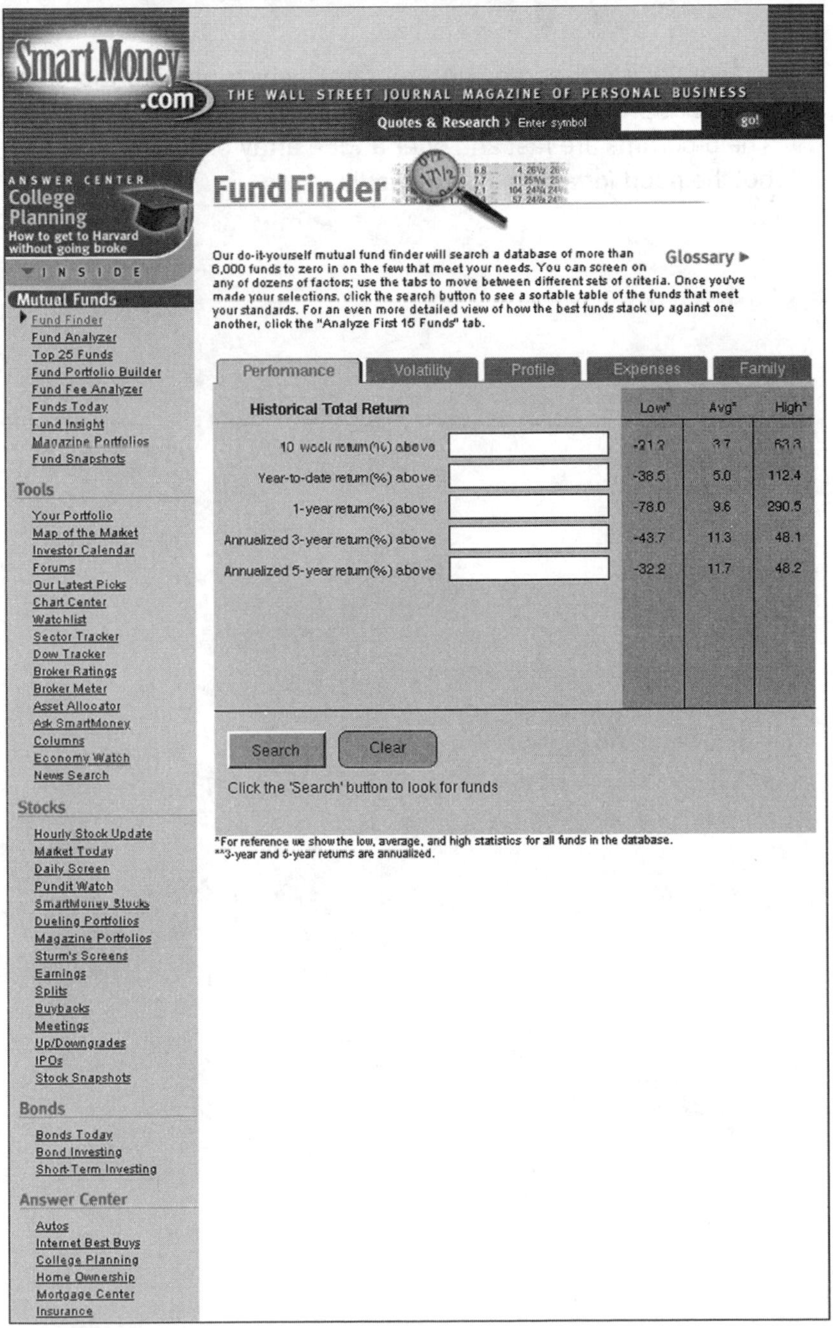

IN A NUTSHELL

Internet stock-screening programs, which provide the same tools that professionals use, are available at several Web sites. The programs are fast and offer a wide array of information without the need for a particular expertise.

CHAPTER 5

Investing in a New Market Environment

The objective of long-term investing is the accumulation of wealth, which in turn depends on achieving an optimal rate of return on your invested assets. The four dimensions to investment return are *reward, risk, cost,* and *time.* All four dimensions are interlinked; weighing each of them properly in light of the goals you want to achieve is the key to any sound investment program and deserves your special attention.

Reward

Reward has be placed first as a factor in the process of wealth accumulation. Looking back over the past few years, during which the stock market, with an annualized return of a spectacular 30 percent, has turned each $100,000 of equity value into $220,000, building assets has seemed easy. During the great bull market that began on August 20, 1982, and continued through the end of 1998, the market advanced at an annual rate of 20 percent, an even more astonishing rate sustained over a period of 16 years. During this boom period, each $100,000 of initial equity value increased to $1.6 million!

Financial markets, however, have demonstrated a remarkable tendency to revert to the mean over time. The U.S. stock market, measured since 1801 (almost two centuries), has been no exception. University of Pennsylvania Professor Jeremy J. Siegel, in his book *Stocks for the*

Long Run, notes that the real (after inflation) returns on equities have averaged 6.7 percent annually. Over 25-year measurement periods, the high range of real returns (9 to 11 percent) came in the periods ending in the 1880s, 1950s, and 1960s. The low range (below 4 percent) came in the late 1850s, the 1930s, and (believe it or not) during all the 25-year periods ending in the 1980s, when high inflation sharply eroded very good nominal returns. All that glitters is not gold!

The real return during the past 25 years has been exactly 6.7 percent, according to Professor Siegel. So perhaps we are merely living in a normal era. But it would be unwise to lose sight of the fact that the 12.8 percent *real* return of the past 15 years—almost double the long-term norm—has only been exceeded in half a dozen of the 181 periods of like duration since 1801. In light of that fact, many investors are reevaluating the question of whether U.S. stocks should remain the predominant asset class in the allocation of an investment portfolio today.

One thing seems clear: The investment fundamentals are far less attractive today than in mid-1982, when the bull rampage began. Then, stocks were priced at a multiple of 7.9 times earnings. In early 1999 at 25.0 times earnings, they are more than three times as richly valued. Then, one dollar of dividends could be purchased for $16 (a yield of 6 percent). Now, with the yield at 1.4 percent, a dollar of dividends costs $71—almost four times as richly valued. Dividends may not matter anymore (or, as it could happen, they may), but if a price of $71 is not too high, there must be *some* price that is too high to pay for that dollar.

Irrespective of what the future holds, however, it seems to the author that equities should remain the investment of choice for the long-term investor. Those who believe the market's incredible momentum and cash flow will continue, and accept the thesis that we are indeed in a new era of global growth, will hold the line in their equity allocation. But those who believe that such fundamentals as earnings and dividends matter and that, in the fullness of time, historic norms will prevail should be at least slightly wary of the powerful wind driving the high returns in this great bull market. There's no way to be sure whether we have been experiencing an asset-price bubble, but in the financial markets it's always wise to expect the unexpected.

Risk

The second dimension of investment return is risk—one of the hallmarks of equity investing. Looked at simply, it is the uncertainty of return. Many investors use statistics to provide a measurable definition of risk. This definition measures variability, the amount by which your investment return could vary around the expected average return. For example, suppose a five-year certificate of deposit has a guaranteed 6 percent return over the holding period. Because the 6 percent return is guaranteed, there is no other possible realized return and therefore no variability—the risk is zero.

Now suppose you are presented with a second potential investment that has a 50 percent chance of a 40 percent return and a 50 percent chance of a 10 percent loss over the holding period. The mathematically expected return on this second investment is 15 percent [(50% × 40%) + (50% × –10%)]. But the actual return may be different from the expected return of 15 percent. We see here the existence of risk. The greater the potential variability, the greater the risk.

Potential variability can be used to compare the riskiness of different investments and to make judgments about the suitability of a particular investment for your portfolio, taking into consideration your own level of comfort for risk. In practical terms, you often will determine the riskiness of a particular investment subjectively, using research and other information available to you.

However, in comparing the 6 percent guaranteed, no-risk investment with the investment whose expected return of 15 percent has some risk, we aren't able to say which is the better investment. Higher return means higher risk. The investment choice depends on the trade-off between risk and return that you're willing to make. Your objectives should be considered in terms of both reward and risk. In an efficient market, expected returns will be higher for securities that have higher degrees of risk.

How long you hold your securities has an important impact on the risk and return trade-off. For example, the risk and return trade-off for a one-year holding period will be different from the trade-off for a five-year holding period. Stock market risk tends to decline as the holding period lengthens. Therefore, setting a proper time frame is very important when making investment decisions.

The two components of the risk that an investor faces are:

1. *Market risk,* which is inherent in the market itself
2. *Company risk,* which involves the unique characteristics of any one stock or bond and the industry in which it operates

About 70 percent of the risk you face as an investor is company risk. Fortunately, you can eliminate this risk by diversifying among different securities. For example, you can invest in ten different stocks or bonds rather than just one.

Market risk is the other 30 percent of total risk and cannot be avoided by diversification, for all stocks and bonds are affected to some degree by the overall market.

The fact that you eliminate company risk simply by diversifying your portfolio is critical to the long-term success of your investment strategy. An investor who owns just one stock is taking on 100 percent of the risk associated with investing in common stocks, whereas an investor with a diversified portfolio has only 30 percent of that risk. Put differently, a single-stock investor has more than three times the risk of a diversified investor.

Investors who think of themselves as conservative but who invest in one low-risk stock actually incur more risk than investors who have a portfolio of ten aggressive growth stocks. In addition, the conservative investors are getting a lower expected return, for they are invested in lower-risk, lower-return stocks.

This brings us to an important investment concept. The stock and bond markets provide higher returns for higher risks, but they provide those higher returns only for unavoidable risk. *Company risk is mostly avoidable through diversification.* Regardless of what investment objective you may have, what your intended holding period is, or what kind of securities analysis is performed, if you do not have a diversified portfolio, you are either throwing away return or assuming risk that could be avoided (or dramatically reduced), or both.

For adequate diversification, your portfolio should contain at least ten different stocks or bonds, with approximately equal dollar amounts in each. In buying stocks, select companies that appear to offer the greatest chance for future earnings expansion.

Cost

The first two elements of reward and risk are the accepted dimensions of investment returns. But another critical factor in returns, comparable to the depth that gives a geometrical figure its third dimension, is cost. And its impact on reward and risk cannot be overstated.

Cost can be looked at as a simple reduction of gross return. A mutual fund investment program with a return of 10 percent earned by a manager who receives a fee of ¼ of 1 percent provides the investor with a net return of 9¾ percent, whereas the same return from a manager charging ¾ of 1 percent provides the investor with 9¼ percent. A long-term investor looking at a compound interest table will immediately note that $100,000 invested over a 25-year period in the former case yields a terminal value of $910,000; in the latter, $1,020,000. That $110,000 difference exceeds the entire initial investment. And if, in the long run, gross returns of managers—good and bad, lucky and unlucky alike—tend to regress to the market mean, cost must become a vital element when you consider which fund to buy. More than parenthetically, note that the entire 10 percent market return (if you are managing your own portfolio without professional management) would produce $1,080,000 over 25 years.

Although cost matters in every far-flung corner of the world of investing, it matters most where it is the highest. The exceptionally high purchase fees and management costs that characterize much of the mutual fund industry and the high commissions of full-service and some discount stock brokers mean that returns earned by investors are extremely sensitive to cost.

I cannot imagine that any reasonably intelligent investor seeking to put his or her capital to work would select one of the mutual funds in the high-cost category or select a fund with a sales load. But consider the impact of even average costs, 2 percent annually, on a long-term investment in mutual funds. Although, as noted earlier, a 10 percent market gross return would carry $100,000 to $1,080,000 in 25 years, the commensurate fund's net return of 8 percent would provide but $680,000. Surely, when a full market risk is assumed, receiving 63 percent of the market's terminal value is hardly an adequate reward.

So far we have addressed only a portion of the cost issue—investment expenses. But taxes can take an even greater toll on your taxable investment returns. Mutual funds, for instance, are notoriously inefficient from a tax standpoint. Their portfolios are typically managed with utter disregard for tax considerations. Annual portfolio turnover averages 90 percent, equivalent to owning a brand-new list of holdings every 13 months. The penalty would be serious even if the resulting gains were subject to today's maximum 20 percent tax rate on long-term gains. But in 1997, according to The Vanguard Group, about 30 percent of mutual fund gains were short term in duration (39.6 percent maximum tax rate) and 20 percent were midterm (28 percent rate). Thus, the approximate 8 percent capital gains distribution paid by the average fund would have penalized returns by fully 2.2 percentage points. It is worth noting that the average equity fund actually lagged the market during the year by an amazing 6.1 percentage points *before* taxes.

Time

The fourth dimension in successful investing is time. Albert Einstein has often been quoted as having described compound interest as "the greatest mathematical discovery of all time." Mutual fund marketers make the most of the quote (if indeed he did actually say it), using compound interest to illustrate the increasing capital value accruing to stocks over time, often comparing equities with fixed interest savings. In a typical long-term—say, 40-year—chart, a mutual fund line might show a $10,000 investment in equities with an assumed 12 percent return, and another line would show savings of $10,000 growing with an interest return of 5 percent. The savings plan limps along to a final value of $70,000. But the equity plan soars to $930,000. The value of time—the fourth dimension of return—shows dramatic results.

But long-term investing has been honored more in theory than in action. In the mutual fund industry, managers clearly invest for the short term, with nearly one-half of equity fund portfolios having turnover of more than 100 percent each year. The typical mutual fund investor thinks short term too. The average shareholder holds mutual funds for less than three years. On the other hand, wealthy private investors have the lowest turnover of any large group (perhaps explaining why they are wealthy in the first place).

IN A NUTSHELL

Successful investors apply four interdependent basic dimensions that affect long-term return to every asset class in which they participate. *Reward* and *risk* go hand-in-hand. *Cost* can have a significant impact on either—or both. And because lengthening duration accelerates aggregate rewards, reduces volatility risk, and magnifies the burden of costs, time interacts with all three of the other factors.

Preparing Your Own
Personal Financial Plan

Despite the uncertainty of the stock market, investments remain a topic of choice among the baby boom generation (and others). Your money has to go somewhere, and under the mattress won't cut it.

How much do you need, and what investments should you choose to be able to retire to that golf community in Florida or beach cottage of your dreams? An entire industry of investment firms and financial planners is ready to counsel you, often for a hefty fee or big commissions on security purchases, but budget-minded, do-it-yourself investors are turning to inexpensive software that assesses their investments, tells them how much money they will need in retirement, and provides guidelines on investing to meet that goal. This chapter focuses first on the software to help you get started, then on sound investment principles that will enable you to reach your financial goals.

A number of excellent programs you can run on your computer are available. The best are simple, harvesting data from an electronic checkbook to give you an accurate thumbnail appraisal of saving and spending habits that will put you on track for that house along the fairway. The worst resemble an Internal Revenue Service audit. Your experience with them depends largely on your recordkeeping and financial acumen. If you already have a program like Quicken or Microsoft Money and keep detailed financial records, projecting your future will be easy. If you keep old bills in a shoe box, you're in for many hours of tedious data entry. If you let your records pile up because you don't know how to organize your finances, however, you might consider using these programs to help you turn that pile of receipts into a sensible balance sheet and income statement.

Following are some financial planning programs that are worth taking a look at.

Comprehensive Financial Planning Programs

Four of the best computer-driven financial planning programs are:

1. *Quicken Financial Planner,* which can be purchased separately or as part of the popular Quicken Suite
2. *Microsoft Money Financial Suite 99,* which includes Microsoft's Lifetime Planner
3. *Plan Retirement Quick and Easy* from Individual Software, which also makes Retire Ready Deluxe
4. *T. Rowe Price Retirement Planning Analyzer,* which you can get by mail on CD-ROM or can download

These programs prod you through a detailed questionnaire to determine your long-term financial status. The plans forecast and suggest investments based on several factors, such as how fast you want your money to grow, how much risk you want to take, and how various investments (stocks, bonds, mutual funds) have performed over time. Their pie charts telling you how to divide your investments can be found in many financial firms' brochures.

Quicken Financial Planner

Quicken Financial Planner (Intuit, $39.95) takes information from your checkbook to determine your spending and savings habits—provided you already use Quicken's software. The planner won't work with other companies' checkbook files unless you have a full-featured Quicken program that will convert them to a Quicken file first.

Quicken's financial planner is a straightforward workbook with a lot of text that is not always easy to follow. The printed 34-page user's guide is clearer, telling you what to enter at each step as well as what items should wait for later steps. To understand how changing your inflation number will affect your outcome, there is a help button. This planner moves along very methodically.

Microsoft Money Financial Suite 99

Microsoft Money Financial Suite 99 (Microsoft, $64.95) has harnessed the power of multimedia for its financial planner, which has clear prompts throughout the program to help you fill out the forms properly. It takes a little time to grasp the control button layout on the designed page, but it soon becomes clear. The program has a college cost estimator and has impressive "what if" capabilities. In addition, it has drop-down worksheets and calculators for tallying costs on the spot and a quiz that determines your risk tolerance so you can tell if your expected returns are in line with how much risk you can stand.

Plan Retirement Quick and Easy

Plan Retirement Quick and Easy (Individual Software, Inc., $19.95) lives up to its name pretty well, but this no-frills program leaves little latitude for temporary, but large, expenses—like college costs—that people may need to figure in, even if they mainly have retirement on their mind. This program is organized differently from the others. It asks you to lump investments into taxable and tax-deferred ones, and it expects you to know the difference. It offers worksheets at the click of a button to help you get organized but doesn't have a provision for life insurance.

T. Rowe Price Retirement Planning Analyzer

T. Rowe Price Retirement Planning Analyzer (T. Rowe Price, $19.95 on CD-ROM or $9.95 downloaded from www.troweprice.com) starts with a tutorial on why you save, how money grows, and how time and risk affect investments. A fast tutorial demonstrates how to enter numbers and use the controls, so you don't need a manual (but it includes one even if you download the software from the Web). The program moves speedily through personal information in a simple, yet comprehensive, way. But even though the planner starts out assuming that you don't know what risk is in the data entry section, it expects you to have an understanding of asset classes and know other financial basics.

Achieving your financial goals requires a disciplined, systematic approach to investing. You need to know whether you have the right mix of investments for your personal situation. Today you can choose from more than 6,000 stocks and bonds, and more than 8,000 mutual funds. This chapter will help you form your own investment objectives, sort through the huge number of offerings, and develop a well-designed plan for investing.

Long-Term Focus

The long-term focus of your financial plan considers commitments made for five years or more. For example, many investors set retirement and college funding as their high-priority objectives.

Saving, where safety and conservation are important, differs from investing, which involves taking a certain degree of risk with your money in pursuit of higher returns. Investment programs involving stocks, bonds, and mutual funds have delivered higher returns over time than FDIC-insured savings accounts and Treasury bills, but they also decline in value from time to time and are not FDIC-insured.

If you can't tolerate fluctuating values in your assets, you probably should avoid the securities markets. This book is designed for investors who can patiently wait out short-term declines in the stock and bond markets as they pursue potentially higher long-term returns.

Short-Term Needs

Construct your long-term investment program on a savings foundation that holds sufficient funds for short-term needs. Short-term moneys are those that you may need within five years. Goals may include a rainy-day fund for emergencies or savings for a car, vacation, home, or other purpose. Financial planners typically recommend an emergency fund of about six months' worth of living expenses. As much as a year's worth might be appropriate for someone who is self-employed or retired. You can add to that the total of other short-term goals you may have.

Your short-term savings should be accessible and safe. Popular choices for many investors include money market funds, bank certificates of deposit (CDs), T-bills, and short-term bond funds. Bank CDs pay a fixed rate of interest and the principal is guaranteed by an agency of the U.S. government, but you may be subject to a penalty for early withdrawal. Money market fund yields fluctuate and lack a government guarantee but are quickly available and offer competitive market returns. Treasury bills pay a fixed rate of interest and are guaranteed by the U.S. government. Short-term bond funds may pay a little higher return and are an option for investors willing to take a small amount of risk.

Classes of Assets

The most critical step in creating a long-term investment program is to allocate your assets by striking a balance between the three common investment classes:

1. *Cash reserve securities* provide stable investment value and current investment income. This group includes money market funds, T-bills, and bank CDs.
2. *Bonds* are interest-bearing obligations issued by corporations; the federal government and its agencies; and state and local governments. The yields offered by these securities are generally higher than those from cash reserves, but their value fluctuates with bond market conditions.
3. *Common stocks* represent ownership rights in a corporation. They usually pay dividends and offer potential for capital growth, but stock market risk can be substantial.

Your future investment returns depend to a great extent on how you allocate your money among these three classes.

Risk and Return: Discovering the Trade-Off

Common stocks have historically delivered the highest average annual returns of the three investment classes. Since 1926 the average annual return on stocks has been 11 percent. Bonds have had an average return of 5.2 percent and the average return on cash reserves has been 3.7 percent. These percentages represent total return: income or yield plus any capital gain or loss. Over the past 30 years, an investment in stocks would have grown to more than twice the same investment in bonds and three times the same investment in cash reserves.

Although stocks and bonds may offer higher returns than cash reserves, they also expose you to more risk. This is a trade-off: To pursue higher investment returns, you must be willing to assume higher risk.

Inflation risk—the risk that the general increase in the cost of living (inflation) will reduce the real value of your investment—is also important to keep in mind. If the total return on your investment is 10 percent but inflation is 4 percent, your actual or real return is only 6 percent.

Allocating Your Assets— Striking the Right Balance for You

How you divide your savings among cash reserves, bonds, and stocks depends on four factors:

1. Your financial situation
2. Your objectives
3. Your time horizon
4. Your ability to tolerate risk

Of these, perhaps the most important factor is time. The longer you have to invest, the greater the risk you can assume.

Investing for Retirement

If you are investing for retirement, your objective during your working years is to accumulate assets. Your investment plan should emphasize growth. With retirement investing, you have the time to take measured risks. While you are in your 20s, 30s, and even 40s, you have a time horizon extending for decades. After you retire, your objectives include preserving the money that has built up and spending it to support your lifestyle. At that time your investments should emphasize income, with some growth of capital to offset inflation. With today's longer life expectancies, you could still be investing for 20 or 30 years after retirement. Such long spans provide the time to ride out short-term market fluctuations.

With these objectives in mind, your asset allocation for retirement should emphasize stocks when you are young and bonds and cash reserves as you grow older. Of course, always keep separate savings reserved for emergencies and short-term objectives.

Investing for Your Children's Education

In some ways, investing for college is similar to investing for retirement. When your child is young, your objective is to achieve maximum growth of your capital. Then when your child enters college, you need ready access to your money as various bills come due. At the same time, your education fund should continue to earn a reasonable return.

Of course, an education plan has a different, shorter time frame than a retirement plan does. If your child begins college at age 18 for an undergraduate degree, the time is about 22 years. Once your child enters the teenage years, little time is left to recoup possible investment losses that may occur. The shorter the time left until college entry, the less risk you should take with your investments.

As in retirement planning, your asset allocation for college investments should emphasize stocks during the early years, when your child is young, then turn more conservative when your child enters the teen years. In the final span, your college investments should consist mainly of money market instruments and short-term bonds.

Allocating Assets at Different Ages

By diversifying your portfolio of securities, you can easily strike a beneficial investment balance to fulfill your objectives. If you are 20 to 50 years old, having a growth objective to build your retirement fund is appropriate. When you near retirement, from age 50 to age 60, move to a balanced growth approach to reduce the risk of large losses. Then in early retirement, spread some assets into cash reserves to protect capital even more while maintaining conservative growth. During your later years, you'll be more concerned about current income than about growth, so you can then transfer more funds from stocks to bonds.

Which Types of Investments Should You Choose?

Once you've decided how to allocate your assets to meet your long-term objectives, the next step is to select specific investments. Consider a number of important issues in planning your investment portfolio. (Other chapters in this book cover each issue in some detail.) Following are the main aspects you should consider in your decision.

Stocks

Stocks are generally divided into *growth stocks* and *value stocks.* You can purchase growth stocks when your objective is capital gains; buy value stocks when you want dividend income. Growth stocks are recommended for portfolios in which growth and balanced growth are the major objectives. Value stocks appeal more to older or more conservative investors whose portfolios are geared to conservative growth and income. Many stocks are further subdivided into such groups as aggressive growth, growth and income, income, and small company.

Bonds

Bonds vary according to risk and duration. In choosing a bond, consider the following questions:

- *How much risk are you willing to assume?* In general, the higher the income yield a bond pays, the greater the risk.
- *Should you investigate the benefits of tax-exempt versus taxable bonds?* Investors in the top tax bracket can receive income that is exempt from both federal and state taxes.

Other Stocks and Bonds

- *International stocks and bonds* can provide additional diversification but are subject to currency fluctuations and other risks.
- *Small company stocks* have the potential for higher returns but entail greater risk from stock market volatility.
- *Specific industry stocks* possibly offer higher returns from high-growth areas such as biotechnology, computers, or the Internet.
- *Junk bonds* produce higher yields but at significantly greater risk because of their lower credit quality.

Designing Your Investment Strategy

Timing Your Investments

Some investors pursue a strategy of attempting to time the market. This involves moving in and out of stocks and bonds, hoping to buy when prices are low and sell when prices are high, with a goal of avoiding market declines. Unfortunately, few investors (if any) can accurately foresee the direction of the stock or bond markets.

Dollar Cost Averaging

This strategy avoids the pitfalls of market timing. Under a dollar cost averaging program, you invest a certain dollar amount on a regular schedule, regardless of market conditions. If you're investing in mutual funds, the plan can be implemented by using electronic transfers from your checking account to your fund, by automatic transfers from a money market fund, through payroll deductions in an employer-sponsored retirement plan, or by simply mailing a check each month to your fund.

As Chapter 10 shows, dollar cost averaging can be critical to your achieving long-term investment success.

Common Mistakes to Avoid

Try to avoid these four common mistakes whether you are investing in stocks, bonds, or mutual funds:

1. *Buying the most recent best performer.* In any market environment, some stocks and mutual funds have produced phenomenal returns. Unfortunately, too often last year's best performers can become this year's laggards. Special market conditions can make particular stocks act like shooting stars—but like these stars, they can fade as suddenly as they appeared. In the same way, aggressive or specialty techniques can rocket a fund to the top one year, then lead it to a dizzying decline the next. Stocks and mutual funds that consistently perform well year in, year out tend to end up in the top 10 percent over a decade or longer.

2. *Acting on intuition and hunches.* Few people are able to accurately forecast market trends. You'll be better off developing a consistent, disciplined approach to investing and sticking to it. Successful investors who endure practice discipline and consistency.

3. *Overdiversifying.* Diversification is a primary attribute of successful investing. But purchase and sale commissions make it costly for an investor of limited means to buy only a few shares of dozens of stocks. Often it makes more sense to buy a mutual fund and obtain instant cost-effective diversification. In the same way, investors who own dozens of mutual funds (which as a whole behave like the market) can save themselves a lot of

trouble by buying a low-cost index fund. (For more on index funds, see Chapter 28.)

4. *Selling too soon.* Investment cycles tend to go in and out of favor. During some years the market will favor growth stocks, small company stocks, or undervalued stocks. When a style goes out of favor for several years, stock performance in that group will suffer, but the stocks in that group will also rebound when the style returns to favor. The danger you face as an investor is selling a stock or fund right before its performance improves in favor of a security whose performance is about to weaken.

Other Considerations

Always know the *costs* of investing in a potential security or mutual fund. Because costs necessarily reduce investment returns, lower costs inevitably mean higher returns.

Consider *taxes* in your investment planning. Investing in a tax-deferred individual retirement account (IRA) or company-sponsored 401(k) plan can have an important long-term effect on your investment return. Also consider the taxability of income and capital gains distributions as well as the tax effect of going in and out of securities investments.

If you are evaluating a mutual fund, one factor to consider is its *past performance.* Remember, though, the caveat that applies to every mutual fund: Past performance is not necessarily an indication of future income or total return.

IN A NUTSHELL

Achieving your financial goals requires a disciplined, systematic approach to investing and the right mix of investments for your personal situation. To help you form your own investment objectives and develop a well-designed plan for investing, try one of the excellent financial planning programs you can run on your computer. Then apply sound investment principles to take you to your goals.

Online Scams and the Greater Fool Theory

The Internet is as an excellent tool for investors, allowing them to easily and inexpensively research investment opportunities. But the Internet is also an excellent tool for swindlers. That's why you should always think twice *before* you invest your money in any opportunity you learn about through the Internet.

In an attempt to fight stock fraud on the Internet, the Securities and Exchange Commission (SEC) has trained a group of "cybercops" to look for scams and illegal trading activity. Little more than a month after it announced the formation of the Office of Internet Enforcement in 1998, SEC officials had trained more than 100 investigators to stop stock scams and price manipulations that leave unsuspecting investors with little or no money in their accounts.

Known as the Cyberforce, these inspectors periodically surf the Net for leads on companies and individuals suspected of illegally trying to influence the price of stocks. With market volatility at its highest point in recent years, SEC officials said the timing is perfect for rogue brokers and stock issuers to use the Internet to find individuals willing to invest money with the promise of a big return. "Fraud on the Internet can proceed very efficiently," according to John Reed Stark, the SEC's top cybercop. His inspectors continuously scan message boards, chat rooms, and other postings on the Net to discover the people involved in unscrupulous practices.

In October 1998, the SEC announced charges against 44 stock promoters caught in a nationwide enforcement sweep to combat Internet fraud. These promoters failed to tell investors that more than 235 companies paid them millions of dollars in cash and shares in exchange for touting their stock on the Internet. "Not only did they lie about their own independence, some of them lied about the companies they featured, then took advantage of any quick spike in price to sell their shares for a fast and easy profit," said SEC Director of Enforcement Richard H. Walker. About 130 complaints are received by the SEC's Enforcement Complaint Center every day from people asking the agency to investigate companies, individuals, and sometimes fellow investors. The SEC also has teamed up with other law enforcement agencies, such as the FBI, to build criminal cases against companies and individuals.

The SEC has seen several cases of "pump-and-dump" frauds, in which a group of individuals pump a stock relentlessly to drive it up and then sell it all at the same time, taking home hefty portions of inflated profits. Officials also have seen an increase in pyramid and Ponzi schemes through the Internet. In Ponzi schemes, original investors are paid massive returns from funds from later investors, who end up losing all or most of their money.

Efforts also are being made in the private sector to combat the bad guys. SRA International, in a partnership with Integralis and Sequel Technology Corporation, has developed a new technology like a search engine to assist the securities industry in identifying falsely hyped stock information on the Internet. This technology protects financial institutions from the illegal passing of misleading stock information by searching for such trouble phrases as *hot stock* and *guaranteed investment* and then flagging these messages. The system also monitors chat rooms, newsgroups and Web sites that push technology services.

A Case in Point

No legislative action can prevent a fool from being parted from his or her money—an unfortunate fact that many investors learn the hard way. Two weeks after the SEC spotlighted how grifters work classic cons on the Web, duping eager investors, an incident occurred that rapidly drove up the price of an obscure stock until the Nasdaq pulled the plug.

No evidence of wrongdoing by the company involved was found, but the meteoric rise and fall in a single day of an obscure, unprofitable California network provider called AvTel Communications, Inc., amid vague claims of a phantom business advantage underscores the dangers of trading in a hyperactive and highly technical market, while also reminding us of the valuable role that established markets can play in rationalizing fast-moving trading.

The case started at 10:26 AM on November 12, 1998, when someone calling himself dennismenis99 posted the same message in a dozen Yahoo! Finance discussion groups devoted to the hottest Internet stocks on the market.

"Hot news: AVCO going up! Next EBAY!" the poster declared on the Ebay board, comparing Santa Barbara–based AvTel (Nasdaq: AVCO), a provider of broadband network services for individuals and corporate customers, to the Internet auction site that had gained more than 100 points in the preceding month.

Within 20 minutes, dennismenis99 had posted virtually identical messages in discussion groups devoted to other highfliers such as Lycos, Egghead Software, K-Tel International, RealNetworks, Onsale, Dell Computers, CDNow, Yahoo!, Ciena, Think New Ideas, and Infoseek, hyping AvTel as an Internet stock.

Each message repeated the same details from an overheated AvTel press release. Touting the launch to about 10,000 Santa Barbara customers of high-speed Internet access over Asymmetric Digital Subscriber lines (ADSLs), it declared: "ADSL is a new modem-based technology that provides a dedicated connection to the Internet that is up to 50 times faster than conventional modems. It works on an existing phone line and allows the sending and receiving of voice and data simultaneously. The user is always just a click away from the Net with no wait and no busy signals." The press release carried the headline: "50 Times Faster Than Conventional Modems? Now That's Fast!"

With the stock market already blindly consuming everything Internet-related, this statement was like throwing raw meat into a feeding frenzy of wolves. By noon the stock price had jumped from just over $2 a share to nearly $10 a share. By early afternoon the price of the stock was above $12. Then, shortly after 3:30 PM, the company was mentioned favorably on CNBC. AvTel rocketed to $31 a share at the close.

Late in the afternoon the short sellers arrived. (Short sellers borrow shares of a stock from brokers, speculating that its price will decline, then make good on the borrowed shares with new ones purchased—they hope—at the lower price.) Almost immediately the short sellers were taunting the gullible about the inevitable crash and flooding the boards with messages of doom, trying to drive the price down. At 5:40 PM, the Nasdaq exchange finally pulled the plug, halting trading and requesting additional information from the company—but not before its stock price nudged up to $38 in after-hours trading. All told, in just eight hours AvTel's stock price had risen 1,278 percent on a volume of 3.6 million shares compared with a daily average of 3,300 shares. Nasdaq's big concern was AvTel's press release, which misled many investors, perhaps unintentionally.

Even though ADSL is indeed faster than conventional modems and allows simultaneous transmissions of voice and data, it was not new technology—many companies around the world were already testing it—and AvTel does not have a proprietary interest in its development. The company neither makes the modems nor seems to have plans to deploy the technology beyond its very limited market in Santa Barbara. By that standard, any company experimenting with the ADSL technology could have issued the same press release and with no greater prospects of future windfalls should ADSL catch on big.

When the Nasdaq exchange allowed trading to resume on Monday, November 16, AvTel opened at just over $3 a share, almost back to where it had started the previous Thursday and barely up from its 52-week low of $1.75. During the day, it enjoyed a brief bounce, kicking the stock's price into the low teens, but then it began a slow, steady skid. On Wednesday, it closed at $8^{23}/_{32}$. In early 1999 the stock was trading at $6 a share.

The Nasdaq exchange has neither confirmed nor denied whether it is investigating the AvTel volatility, although at least three law firms have filed class action lawsuits against AvTel. For its part, the company has made no statement on the bizarre affair.

In many ways, the AvTel story has the signs of a classic pump-and-dump, where scamsters overhype a stock, often because they want to dump it, using high-pressure sales, illusions of investor interest, and bogus information. Just when individuals start buying and thus drive up the price, the con artists dump the shares they bought at much lower prices, often sending the price of the stock back to zero. Face it, anyone who owned a pile of $2 shares could have cleaned up big that day.

In this case, the megahyped Internet stock environment and AvTel's publicity on CNBC launched the stock into the stratosphere, but it took the volatile combination of the oddball press release, an army of investors hungry for a piece of an Internet superstar, and some suspicious, still unidentified hucksters loitering in cyberspace to light the rocket.

How could so many investors be fooled by such a thinly veiled hype spun by an anonymous poster with a frankly ridiculous handle? The SEC warned in an October 1998 press release how to spot Internet stock scams, noting that a "single person can easily create the illusion of widespread interest in a small, thinly traded stock by posting a series of messages under various aliases." While dennismenis99 may or may not have been just one person, technology made it possible to target the intended eager audience narrowly and instantaneously, homing in on investors already focused on other stocks whose value was shifting.

The bulletin boards where investors eagerly trade tips on hot issues have the potential to exert enormous influence on the performance of individual stocks, as was clearly (and painfully) demonstrated in the AvTel disaster. Like Ebay before it, the number of messages in the Yahoo! Finance discussion group exploded after poking along at just a few each month. Many of the messages during the days of the debacle were euphoric as the stock took off, then confused when the Nasdaq pulled the plug, and dismayed when the stock fell back to earth. But at the same time, hundreds of the messages were clearly opportunistic, shamelessly touting other stocks as—you guessed it—"the next AVCO." The message board was at times abusive, littered with misinformation about the Nasdaq's actions, the business of stock trading, and the company itself.

The moral of the story? At a time when a stock trade is just a click away, a lot of naïve and overeager investors—and some market makers—took a bath when they got caught up in the momentum of a stock simply because someone attached the word *Internet* to it. They were willing to buy a stock at any price so long as it was heading skyward. The theory: There will always be a greater fool down the line that will pay more.

Where the Frauds Are

The Internet allows individuals or companies to communicate with a large audience without spending a lot of time, effort, or money. Anyone can reach tens of thousands of people by building an Internet Web site, posting a message on an online bulletin board, entering a discussion in a live chat room, or sending mass e-mails. It's easy for swindlers to make their messages look real and credible. But it's nearly impossible for investors to tell the difference between fact and fiction.

Online Investment Newsletters

Hundreds of online investment newsletters have appeared on the Internet in recent years. Many offer investors seemingly unbiased information free of charge about featured companies or recommend monthly stock picks. Legitimate online newsletters can help investors gather valuable information, but some online newsletters are tools for fraud.

Some companies pay the people who write online newsletters cash or securities to tout their stocks. Although this isn't illegal, federal securities law requires newsletters to disclose who paid them, the amount, and the type of payment; but many swindlers fail to do so. Instead, they lie about the payments they received, their independence, their so-called research, and their track records. Their newsletters masquerade as sources of unbiased information, when in fact they stand to profit handsomely if they convince investors to buy or sell particular stocks.

Some online newsletters falsely claim to independently research the stocks they profile. Others spread false information or promote worthless stocks. The most notorious sometimes scalp the stocks they hype, driving up the price of the stock with their baseless recommendations and then selling their own holdings at high prices and high profits.

Bulletin Boards

Online bulletin boards—whether newsgroups, Usenet, or Web-based bulletin boards—have become an increasingly popular forum for investors to share information. Bulletin boards typically feature threads that are made up of numerous messages on various investment opportunities. Although some messages may be true, many turn out to be bogus—or even scams. Defrauders often pump up a company or pretend to reveal inside information about upcoming announcements, new products, or lucrative contracts.

In addition, you never know for certain who you're dealing with—or whether they're credible—because many bulletin boards allow users to hide their identity behind multiple aliases. People claiming to be unbiased observers who have carefully researched the company may actually be company insiders, large shareholders, or paid promoters. A single person can easily create the illusion of widespread interest in a small, thinly traded stock by posting a series of messages under various aliases.

E-Mail Spam

Because "spam"—junk e-mail—is so cheap and easy to create, swindlers use it increasingly to find investors for bogus investment schemes or to spread false information about a company. Spam allows the unscrupulous to target many more potential investors than cold calling or mass mailing. Using a bulk e-mail program, spammers can send personalized messages to thousands, and even millions, of Internet users at a time.

How to Use the Internet to Invest Wisely

If you want to invest wisely and steer clear of frauds, you must get the facts. Never, ever, make an investment based solely on what you read in an online newsletter or bulletin board posting, especially if the investment involves a small, thinly traded company that isn't well known. And don't even think about investing on your own in small companies that don't file regular reports with the SEC unless you're willing to investigate each company thoroughly and check the truth of every statement about the company. For instance, you'll need to

- get financial statements from the company and be able to analyze them;
- verify the claims about the new product developments or lucrative contracts;
- call every supplier or customer of the company and ask if they really do business with the company; and
- check out the people running the company and find out if they have ever made money for investors before.

A Sampling of Recent SEC Cases

The SEC actively investigates allegations of Internet investment fraud and has, in many cases, taken quick action to stop scams. They also have coordinated with federal and state criminal authorities to put

Internet cheaters in jail. Here are a few recent cases in which the SEC took action:

- *Francis A. Tribble* and *Sloane Fitzgerald, Inc.,* sent more than 6 million unsolicited e-mails, built bogus Web sites, and distributed an online newsletter over a ten-month period to promote two small, thinly traded microcap companies. Because they failed to tell investors that the companies they were touting had agreed to pay them in cash and securities, the SEC sued both Tribble and Sloane to stop them from violating the law again and imposed a $15,000 penalty on Tribble. Their massive spamming campaign triggered the largest number of complaints to the SEC's online Enforcement Complaint Center.

- *Charles O. Huttoe* and 12 other defendants secretly distributed to friends and family nearly 42 million shares of Systems of Excellence Inc., known by its ticker symbol SEXI. In this classic pump-and-dump scheme, Huttoe drove up the price of SEXI shares through false press releases claiming nonexistent multi-million-dollar sales, an acquisition that had not occurred, and revenue projections that had no basis in reality. He also bribed codefendant SGA Goldstar to tout SEXI to subscribers of SGA Goldstar's online *Whisper Stocks* newsletter. The SEC fined Huttoe $12.5 million, but he had spent most of his ill-gotten gains, and investors didn't get their money back. Huttoe and Theodore R. Melcher, Jr., the author of the online newsletter, were sentenced to federal prison. In addition, four of Huttoe's cohorts pled guilty to criminal charges.

- *Matthew Bowin* recruited investors for his company, Interactive Products and Services, in a direct public offering done entirely over the Internet. He raised $190,000 from 150 investors. But instead of using the money to build the company, Bowin pocketed the proceeds and bought groceries and stereo equipment. The SEC sued Bowin in a civil case, and the district attorney's office in Santa Cruz (California) prosecuted him on criminal charges. He was convicted of 54 felony counts and sentenced to ten years in jail.

- *IVT Systems* solicited investments to finance the construction of an ethanol plant in the Dominican Republic. The Internet solicitations promised a return of 50 percent or more with no reasonable basis for the prediction. The literature contained lies about contracts with well-known companies and omitted other important information for investors. After the SEC filed a complaint, the company agreed to stop breaking the law.

- *Gene Block* and *Renate Haag* were caught offering prime bank securities, a type of security that doesn't even exist. They collected over $3.5 million by promising to double investors' money in four months. The SEC has frozen their assets and stopped them from continuing their fraud.

IN A NUTSHELL

With market volatility at its highest point in recent years, the timing is perfect for rogue brokers and fraudulent stock issuers to use the Internet to find individuals willing to invest money with the promise of a big return. At the same time, scam artists take every opportunity to manipulate the market in thinly traded stocks, trapping naïve and unwary investors and leaving them with little or no money in their accounts.

CHAPTER 8

Tips for Online Investors

The Internet and other new technologies are in many ways transforming how our capital markets operate. There are clear benefits for you from these changes, including lower costs and faster access to the markets. But it is important to remember the investment basics and not allow the ease and speed with which you can trade lull you either into a false sense of security or encourage you to trade too often.

Every day, more and more Americans are investing in the stock market, and many of them are doing so through the Internet. Online brokerage accounts for about 25 percent of all retail stock trades. And the number of online brokerage accounts is expected to exceed 10 million by the end of 1999.

Although the manner in which orders are executed may be changing, the time-honored principles of evaluating a stock have not. Your consideration of the fundamentals of a company—net earnings, price-earnings ratios, the products and services offered by the company—should never lose their underlying importance.

Investing in the stock market—however you do it and however easy it may be—will always entail risk. Don't shortcut or bypass the three golden rules for all investors:

1. Know what you are buying.
2. Know the ground rules under which you buy and sell a stock or bond.
3. Know the level of risk you are undertaking.

Online investors should remember that it is just as easy, if not more so, to lose money through the click of a button as it is to make it.

Issues to Be Aware Of

Every online investor should be aware of a number of issues. First, you must understand the issues and limitations of online investing. You may occasionally experience delays on these systems. Demand has grown so quickly that many firms have been racing to keep up with it. Software problems at the online brokerage firm E*TRADE (www.etrade.com) caused its trading system to shut down temporarily for three consecutive days in February 1999. You also may have trouble getting online or receiving timely confirmations of trade executions. You shouldn't always expect instantaneous execution and reporting. There can and will be delays in electronic systems. You should understand options and alternatives to executing and confirming your orders if you encounter online problems.

Second, you may sometimes be surprised at how quickly stock prices actually move. For example, many technology stocks have had dramatic and rapid price movements recently. When many investors attempt to purchase (or sell) the same stock at the same time, the price can move very quickly. Just because you see a price on your computer screen doesn't mean that you will always be able to get that price in a rapidly changing market. Take precautions to ensure that you don't end up paying much more for a stock than you intended or can afford.

One way to protect yourself is to use limit orders rather than market orders when submitting a trade in a hot stock. Investors who don't limit their risk can be subject to surprising results. Say you wanted to buy a stock in an initial public offering (IPO) that was trading earlier at $9, but you failed to specify the maximum you were willing to pay by using a limit order. You could end up paying whatever price the stock has moved to at the time your order reaches the market—$60, $90, or even more. If, on the other hand, you submitted a limit order to buy the stock at $11 or less, the order would be executed only if the market price had not moved past that level. Be sure you understand the risk associated with trading in a rapidly moving market and take all possible actions to control your risk.

Third, investors buying securities on margin may not fully understand the risks involved. In volatile markets, investors who have put up an initial margin payment for a stock may find themselves being required to provide additional cash (maintenance margin) if the price of the stock subsequently falls. If the funds are not paid in a timely manner, the brokerage firm has the right to sell the securities and charge any loss to the investor. When you buy stock on margin, you are borrowing money. And as the stock price changes, you may be required to increase the cash investment. Simply put, you should make sure that you do not overextend.

Fourth, although new technology available to retail investors may resemble that of professional traders, retail investors should exercise caution before imitating the style of trading and risks undertaken by market professionals. For most individuals, the stock market should be used for investment, not trading. Strategies such as day trading can be highly risky, and investors engaging in such activities should do so with money they can afford to lose.

Some Results of Investor Complacency

One of the millions of small investors who have recently flocked to cyberspace placed an order through his online brokerage account for a hot new Internet stock, Theglobe.com, thinking it would cost between $15 and $25 a share. His order was filled for 2,300 shares, at a price of $90 a snare and a bill of $207,000—nearly $150,000 more than he expected.

Another investor placed an order on his personal computer to sell 30 shares of a different company, never got an electronic confirmation, and so placed the sell order again, winding up selling 60 shares, twice the amount of shares he had held.

A third investor tried to cancel an order to buy 45 shares of a stock and received acknowledgment that his cancellation order had been received. But the sale went through anyway, and the investor wound up purchasing the stock.

These three are among hundreds of investors who have complained to the Securities and Exchange Commission (SEC), which has reported that the record amount of online trading—it now constitutes 25 percent of all retail trading and is growing fast—also has brought a record number of complaints. The number of complaints in 1998 rose more than fourfold from 1997.

With new issues of volatile Internet and technology stocks coming to market at prices that are seducing new investors into trying to get rich quick, SEC officials report that the complaints are coming in faster than they can be processed. The growing problems caused Arthur Levitt, the SEC chairman, to caution small investors who have swarmed onto the Internet to approach online investing with care. In addition to keeping the fundamentals of investing in mind, he said, investors should take such precautions as placing limits on the prices of buy and sell orders to avoid the recurring kinds of problems that are plaguing the emerging group of small traders called *cybervestors.* He went on to note that investors need to remember the investment basics and not allow the ease and speed with which they trade to lull them either into a false sense of security or encourage them to trade too quickly or too often. Some of the issues raised specifically relate to online trading, others are generic to all investing. The majority of them can be addressed through better education and by investors doing their homework.

Causes of Online Investing Problems

In part, the problems being encountered by cybervestors demonstrate that technological advances in personal computers and the Internet trail the advances made at the stock exchanges. For example, the stock price that consumers see on the screen may bear no resemblance to the actual real-time price at the exchange—particularly when the stock is volatile or during periods of heavy volume. Those lags have become common with hot new public offerings of technology stocks, whose prices move fast and far.

Some problems are rooted in investor misunderstandings about the new technology. Other problems have been caused by the growing number of neophyte traders, many caught in the speculative fever of recent years. Through the new technology they are able to buy and sell in an instant without any understanding of the risks associated with such highfliers.

The more than 100 brokerage companies now on the Internet have taken different approaches to resolving client complaints. In certain circumstances some companies have been willing to undo the trades, but standards vary greatly from firm to firm and are highly dependent on the specific circumstances and status of the client. And the wave of filings at the regulatory agencies demonstrates that in many cases the companies are not reimbursing customers.

To reduce the problems and also try to insulate themselves from possible liability, many brokerage firms post warnings about trading problems on their Web sites that may be caused by stock volatility and high volume. Those statements had been posted even before the National Association of Securities Dealers (NASD) issued a notice in early 1999 recommending that the firms begin to educate investors and warn them of possible delays and other potential problems.

The SEC has reported that the most common complaints involve investors who bought securities at prices significantly higher than the prices on the screens. Other complaints have come from investors who had moved with a few mouse clicks into securities that, on reflection, they should have never purchased. Still others thought they had canceled purchases before those orders had been executed, only to learn they had not.

Because the stock prices that you see on your computer screen may not necessarily reflect real-time market prices, you should consider the advantages of placing orders that limit the price for a trade to be executed. And always remember the basic principles of investing and understand that as much as the new technology has provided important benefits, it also has shortcomings. Millions of new investors have taken advantage of the unprecedented access and individual control the Internet provides. But new opportunities present new responsibilities, challenges, and risks.

Tips for Trading in Fast-Moving Markets

Investors trading online, who are used to instant access to their account and almost instantaneous executions of their trades, especially need to understand how they can protect themselves in fast-moving markets. Here is a review of important considerations to keep in mind:

- *Online trading is quick and easy, online investing takes time.* With a click of the mouse, you can buy and sell stocks from more than 100 online brokers offering executions as low as $5 per transaction. Although online trading saves you time and money, it does *not* take the homework out of making investment decisions. You may be able to make a trade in a nanosecond, but making wise investment decisions takes time. Before you trade, know why you are buying or selling and the risk of your investment.
- *Set your price limits on fast-moving stocks: market orders versus limit orders.* To avoid buying or selling a stock at a price higher or lower than you wanted, you need to place a limit order rather

than a market order. A limit order is an order to buy or sell a security at a specific price. A buy limit order can only be executed at the limit price or lower, and a sell limit order can only be executed at the limit price or higher. When you place a market order, you can't control the price at which your order will be filled. Remember that your limit order may never be executed because the market price may quickly surpass your limit before your order can be filled. But by using a limit order you also protect yourself from buying the stock at too high a price.

- *Know your options for placing a trade if you are unable to access your account online.* Most online trading firms offer alternatives for placing trades. These alternatives may include Touch-Tone® telephone trades, faxing your order, or doing it the low-tech way— talking to a broker over the phone. Make sure you know whether using these different options may increase your costs. And remember, if you experience delays getting online, you may experience similar delays when you turn to one of these alternatives.

- *If you place an order, don't assume it didn't go through.* Some investors have mistakenly assumed that their orders have not been executed and place another order. They end up either owning twice as much stock as they could afford or wanted or, with sell orders, selling stock they don't own. Talk with your firm about how you should handle a situation in which you're unsure if your original order was executed.

- *If you cancel an order, make sure the cancellation worked before placing another trade.* When you cancel an online trade, it is important to make sure that your original transaction was not executed. Although you may receive an electronic receipt for the cancellation, don't assume that that means the trade was canceled. Orders only can be canceled if they haven't been executed. Ask your firm how you should check if a cancellation order actually worked.

- *If you buy on margin, your broker can sell your securities without a so-called margin call, that is, calling you first to demand money.* Now is the time to reread your margin agreement and pay attention to the fine print. If your account has fallen below the firm's maintenance margin requirement, your broker has the legal right to sell your securities at any time without consulting you first. Some investors have been rudely surprised that margin calls are a courtesy, not a requirement. Brokers are not required to make margin calls to their customers. (For more details, see Chapters 9 and 18.)

Even when your broker offers you time to put more cash or securities into your account to meet a margin call, the broker can act without waiting for you to meet the call. In a rapidly declining market, your broker can sell your entire margin account at a substantial loss to you, because the securities in the account have declined in value.

- *Regulations don't require a trade to be executed within a certain time.* No SEC regulations require a trade to be executed within a set period of time. But if firms advertise their speed of execution, they must not exaggerate or fail to tell investors about the possibility of significant delays.

What to Do If You Have a Complaint

Act promptly. By law, you have only a limited time to take legal action. Follow these steps to solve your problem:

- Talk to your broker or online firm and ask for an explanation. Take notes of the answers you receive.
- If you are dissatisfied with the response and believe that you have been treated unfairly, ask to talk with the broker's branch manager. In the case of an online firm, go directly to the next step.
- If you are still dissatisfied, write to the compliance department at the firm's main office. Explain your problem clearly, and tell the firm how you want it resolved. Ask the compliance office to respond to you in writing within 30 days.
- If you are still not satisfied, then send a letter of complaint to the National Association of Securities Dealers, your state securities administrator, or the Office of Investor Education and Assistance at the SEC along with copies of the letters you have already sent to the firm.

IN A NUTSHELL

Millions of new investors have taken advantage of the unprecedented access and individual control the Internet provides. But new opportunities present us with new responsibilities, challenges, and risks. Remember, investor protection—at its most basic and effective level—starts with the investor. Whether you invest online, on the phone, or in person, know what you are buying, what the ground rules are, and what level of risk you are assuming.

PART TWO

Investment Strategies

Stock Market Strategies

All stock market strategies have but one purpose—to guide you in your quest to realize superior returns on your invested capital. The extraordinary volatility of the securities markets reminds us of how important portfolio planning is to sound long-term investing.

Over the long term (from 1926 to 1998), returns provided by common stocks have averaged +11 percent annually. But this average returns masks a great deal of volatility, as returns from common stocks have fluctuated within a very wide band. In the 73 years from 1926 through 1998, the stock market has provided annual returns ranging from a low of −43.3 percent (in 1931) to a high of +53.9 percent (in 1933).

This extreme volatility is the chief risk of investing in common stocks, but it is a risk that tends to recede from investors' memories after a lengthy period of generally rising stock prices, such as the period that began in August 1982 and continued through early 1999. Those investors new to investing in common stocks may underestimate the volatility in the returns of common stocks because volatility has been muted in recent years.

Time greatly reduces, but does not eliminate, the volatility in returns from stocks. According to Ibbotson Associates, over five-year periods (1926–1930, 1927–1931, and so on) from 1926 through 1998, average returns on stocks ranged from −12.5 percent to +24.8 percent.

Market Approaches

Most strategies used to invest in the stock market fall into one of three general categories:

1. Fundamental analysis
2. Technical analysis
3. Buy and hold the market

Fundamental Analysis

This investment approach is primarily concerned with value. Fundamental analysis examines factors that determine a company's expected future earnings and dividends and the dependability of those earnings and dividends. It then attempts to put a value on the company's stock in accordance with its findings. A fundamentalist then seeks out stocks that are a good value, meaning stocks that are priced low relative to their perceived value. The assumption is that the stock market will later recognize the value of the stock and its price will increase accordingly.

Technical Analysis

The technical analyst attempts to predict the future price of a stock or the future direction of the stock market based on changes in past price and trading volume. This approach assumes that stock prices and the stock market follow discernible patterns, and if the beginning of a pattern can be identified, the balance of the pattern can be predicted well enough to yield returns in excess of the general market. Most academic studies of this approach have concluded that investing based on purely technical analysis does not work.

Buy and Hold the Market

The buy-and-hold-the-market approach is the benchmark against which any other approach to the market should be measured. This strategy provides the returns that would be obtained by buying and holding the stock market, often defined as the S&P 500. Of course, no individual investor would buy all 500 stocks that make up the index (although this can be achieved by buying shares in an S&P 500 index mutual fund, as I discuss later). By investing in a large number of well-diversified stocks, however, investors can build portfolios that closely resemble the S&P 500.

The buy-and-hold-the-market investment approach is used as a benchmark because no other approach based on analysis is valid unless it can outperform the market over the long run. When an investment produces a return that is above the market return with the same risk, the difference between the two returns is referred to as an *excess return.* The excess return represents the added value of the approach.

Buying on Margin

If you feel so optimistic about a stock that you are willing to take on additional risk in the hope of enhancing your return, you can utilize a technique called *buying on margin,* or buying with borrowed funds. According to rules set by the Federal Reserve, brokers can lend you up to half the money you need to buy stocks as long as they have collateral of yours to seize in case your stocks lose value. The collateral must be in the form of securities or cash. The broker will charge you interest on the loan, typically about a percentage point over the prime rate.

By doubling the amount of your purchase (by borrowing), you can make twice as much money if your stock goes up than you can make by paying for your stock in full. But this coin has two sides; if the stock you bought on margin declines in value, you will lose twice as much money as you would if you had paid cash in full. For you to break even, the price of your stock must increase in value by the amount of your interest costs. If the price of your stock drops in half, you will be hit by a margin call—a call from your broker requiring you to put up additional collateral to cover your loan and thus avoid the immediate sale of your position in the stock. If your position is sold, you will have lost your entire investment. Clearly, buying on margin is a risky technique.

Selling Short

Even riskier than buying on margin is a technique called *selling short,* a risk you take if you think the price of a stock will drop. If you are right and your stock does drop in price, you can make a lot of money. But if you are wrong and the stock goes up, your losses are unlimited because the stock you have shorted can rise indefinitely.

Here's the way short selling works: Perhaps you believe the sales of a particular company are slowing dramatically and the company will show a loss at the next reporting period, causing the price of the stock to drop sharply. To sell the stock short, you essentially borrow the shares from someone who owns them, usually your broker, with the promise that you will return the shares later. You then sell the borrowed shares at the current market price, which you think is too high.

When the price drops (congratulations—you were right!), you buy the same number of shares back and return them to the lender. This is known as covering your short position. Your profit is the difference between the price you originally sold the stock for and the price at which you bought it back.

But suppose the company's earnings report turns out to be better than expected and the share price soars—you'll be very unhappy. You must cover your short position, buying the shares back at a higher price than the one at which you sold and taking a loss. The higher the price goes, the greater your loss. Short selling, like buying on margin, should be done only if you have nerves of steel. You can get poor in a hurry if you're wrong.

How Efficient Is the Stock Market?

According to the efficient market theory, the price of a stock in an efficient market reflects all publicly available information concerning that stock and so is extremely close to the true value of the stock. This doesn't mean that a stock's price reflects the stock's true value at all times, but rather that stock prices on average reflect true values. Variations around an average price may exist.

The random walk theory holds that variations in the average price of stocks are unpredictable; sometimes positive and sometimes negative. Because they are unpredictable, they cannot be used to obtain excess returns. This theory concerning random variation in prices purports to explain the short-term price fluctuations that occur seemingly without cause.

Interesting as these two theories are, the question remains: Is the stock market an efficient market? If it is, no point is gained in pursuing the fundamental approach that seeks to find stocks selling significantly above or below their value. The argument would be that stock prices vary randomly around their true value. Investors who believe the stock market is efficient would concentrate on developing a more efficient portfolio rather than concentrating on specific stock selection. An efficient portfolio is one that provides returns closest to the market's return at a given level of market risk. The investor simply determines the amount of risk that he or she is willing to bear and then builds a portfolio accordingly.

Investors who believe the market is inefficient proceed on the assumption that variations in the way people receive and evaluate information cause the prices of some stocks to deviate significantly from their true value. Therefore, they see opportunity in finding underpriced and overpriced stocks through diligent analysis and the ability to outperform a buy-and-hold-the-market strategy.

Based on substantial research evidence, many analysts believe that the market often is inefficient and that there are opportunities for outperforming the market. The excess return potential appears to be in the range of 2 percent to 6 percent annually. Over a lifetime of investing, even a relatively small additional return can lead to substantially additional wealth.

The Effect of Transaction Costs

Don't ignore the impact of transaction costs when comparing the different approaches to investing. Take into account three important factors when trading stocks:

1. Commissions
2. The bid-ask spread
3. Taxes

Let's look at a typical transaction. You own 100 shares of stock in company A and decide to sell them and buy 100 shares of stock in company B. Assume that the last trade on the exchange for each stock was for $25 a share. When you consider these three factors, the cost of making the switch looks something like the following:

Commissions

The total commission cost for selling 100 shares of A and buying 100 shares of B online would be about $15 for each transaction (the range among online firms ranges from $5 to $30). By trading through a broker—offline—the cost would range from $25 to $125. A switch made through an online firm represents a commission of about 1 percent of your $2,500 investment ($2 \times \$15$). Trading through a broker could cost you a lot more.

Bid-Ask Spread

The cost of your switch is increased by the bid-ask spread, which is the difference between the price (bid) at which a stock can be sold and the price (asked) at which it can be bought. For example, for both company A and company B, the current spread may be 24⅞ (bid) to 25⅛ (asked). In this case, you would receive $24.875 a share for selling and pay $25.125 for buying B. You have just suffered another 1 percent charge. The difference between bid and asked prices is the fee retained by the market maker or specialist. An actively traded stock will have a narrower spread than a stock that is thinly traded.

Taxes

If you enjoyed a profit on your sale of company A's stock, you have to pay a tax. Of course, taxes would have to be paid eventually, but if they are deferred (by holding on to the shares), you will continue to earn a return on the eventual liability. Comparing a one-year holding period with a ten-year holding period, the value of deferring taxes could be worth another 0.5 percent each year.

So switching can be expensive. You pay somewhere between 3 and 6 percent to switch from one stock to another. This doesn't mean it shouldn't be done, just that the new stock must perform sufficiently better to overcome the setback. Investors who use investment techniques that result in turning over their entire portfolio several times a year must outperform the market substantially just to match a buy-and-hold approach.

Setting Your Objectives

It's clear that to be successful, you must set an objective in terms of what is to be achieved and the anticipated time frame in which to accomplish the objective.

Short-Term versus Long-Term Risk

· As discussed earlier, how long you hold an investment has an important effect on the degree of risk you undertake. In this context, consider risk as the likelihood that your capital will diminish from the time of your initial purchase to the end of the holding period.

Although the stock market can be risky in the short run, time has a moderating effect, as noted in the beginning of this chapter. The longer you hold a portfolio of stocks, the lower your chances of losing money and the greater the odds of earning a return close to the long-term average.

Real Stock Market Risk

People do, of course, lose money in the market. The following are some of the real risks of investing in the stock market:

- Short-term investing is risky. An investor has about a 30 percent chance of showing a loss at the end of one year. This would happen more often if taxes and transaction costs are figured in.
- Many investors are not sufficiently diversified, taking on more risk and incurring more losses than the market as a whole.
- Many investors speculate ("play the market") in an attempt to make large short-term profits by trading their stocks frequently and by trying to predict short-term market swings (timing the market). Because of high transaction costs, most speculators lose money, even in a market with an overall upward trend.

IN A NUTSHELL

Investing in a diversified portfolio of common stocks offers an outstanding opportunity to accumulate wealth through growth at relatively low risk. The stock market is risky for short-term holding periods and for speculators, but as an investor's holding period goes beyond 5 years, risk is greatly diminished. There have been no losing 15-, 20-, or 25-year periods since 1926.

The All-Time Favorite Investment Technique

Few investment techniques have stood the test of time so well that one can confidently say, "This works." But such a method exists. It's easy, it works, and you can do it. Called *dollar cost averaging,* this plan is simply the practice of buying securities at regular intervals in fixed dollar amounts regardless of price levels.

Small investors have amassed fortunes by making systematic purchases of shares over long periods. For instance, by putting aside as little as $50 each month in mutual funds, you can take advantage of dollar cost averaging, one of the simplest and most effective ways of building an investment portfolio. Larger amounts usually are needed to purchase individual stocks and bonds, but the principle is the same.

When you engage in dollar cost averaging, you purchase more shares at relatively low prices than at high prices. As a result, the average cost of all shares bought turns out to be lower than the average of all the prices at which purchases were made. The combination of buying shares at a variety of price levels and acquiring more shares at low rather than high prices has proven to be an efficient and cost-effective method of accumulating securities.

Average Cost versus Average Price

The arithmetic that illustrates how dollar cost averaging works is simple. You need only remember that by periodically purchasing shares with identical amounts of money and as long as share prices change at all during the investment period, the average cost of shares purchased will be less than the average of the prices paid. For example, say that you decide to invest $280 regularly. You make five purchases totaling $1,400 at prices between $10 and $5 a share. The number of shares bought for each $280 purchase in this example would be as follows (transaction costs are not considered):

Investment	Price	Shares Purchased
$ 280	$10.00	28
280	8.00	35
280	7.00	40
280	5.00	56
280	8.00	35
Total $1,400	$38.00	194

Total shares acquired for $1,400 investment: 194
Average cost of each share ($1,400 divided by 194): $7.22
Average price of shares purchased ($38 divided by 5): $7.60

This program works because an equal number of dollars buys more shares at low prices than at high prices. It is essential that you make purchases at low prices when they are available. If you consider dollar cost averaging, you must take into account your emotional and financial ability to continue making new investments through periods of low price levels.

Dollar cost averaging does not guarantee that you will always have profits in your portfolio or that you will never incur losses. Use an investment program like this only for long-term purposes. You should be pretty sure that you will not need these invested funds for several years.

Dollar cost averaging can substantially reduce the risks inherent in securities investing. Shares are bound to be purchased over the years at a variety of price levels—high, low, and in-between. That fact alone should provide better income and capital gains than haphazard investing or buying only when the outlook appears bright.

Growth Not Essential

Fluctuating security prices are more important to successful dollar cost averaging than long-term growth alone because, surprisingly perhaps, you get your best opportunity to acquire a large number of shares during periods of declining prices.

Continuing the previous example, assume that after you make the five purchases, the share price returns to $10, the level of the first purchase. The 194 shares you already own have a value of $1,940. Your profit is $560. (During the purchase period, we assume that the price had declined as much as 50 percent.)

Now instead of a drop in price, let's see what happens if the share price had steadily advanced to an increase of 50 percent and the five equal purchases of $280 were made, again until the full $1,400 was invested. For this example, let's assume that you purchase fractional shares, as is the case with mutual funds:

	Investment	Price	Shares Purchased
	$ 280	$10.00	28.00
	280	11.00	25.45
	280	12.00	23.33
	280	14.00	20.00
	280	15.00	18.67
Total	$1,400	$62.00	115.45

Total shares acquired for $1,400 investment: 115.45
Average cost of each share ($1,400 divided by 115.45): $12.13
Average price of shares purchased ($62 divided by 5): $12.40

In this example, the process of dollar cost averaging also results in an average cost that is less than the average price. But notice that after a 50 percent increase from the initial price of $10 per share, the total value of the 115.45 shares at $15 is $1,731.75 (115.45 × $15). Although still a profit, the result is about 10.7 percent less than the $1,940 that the 194 shares in the previous example were worth at $10.

Of course, investors have no control over the direction security prices will take once they start a dollar cost averaging program. The plan's main advantage is that in the long run it will work to your benefit almost regardless of what the market does. This is particularly important if you are among those investors who fear starting an investment plan because you believe stock prices are too high. If you are correct and the market does decline, the timing may be just right to begin dollar cost averaging.

Reinvesting Dividends

Many investors who invest in securities on a periodic basis can and do reinvest any dividends they receive. The effect in the beginning is minor, but as the program continues the impact of compounding shares becomes more and more significant. The relative importance will vary, of course, depending on the emphasis that a particular fund company places on paying income distributions on its shares.

Building a fortune by investing in stocks, bonds, or mutual funds, as mentioned earlier, is less a matter of investment skill or luck than of persistence and patience. The first decision to make is whether you truly are willing to forgo immediate gratification to achieve a long-term investment goal. Because the goal is to invest a fixed amount of money on a regular basis for many years, ask yourself the question: "Do I want my dream car today or a fortune tomorrow?"

An Example of Dollar Cost Averaging

Many fine investments are available among stocks, bonds, and mutual funds. Here I'll show you how dollar cost averaging would have worked for an investor who started such a program at age 35 and continued it until retirement at 65, making investments of $5,000 at the beginning of each year from 1969 to 1998 in a portfolio of stocks replicating the Standard & Poor's 500-stock index (S&P 500). In effect, he simply "bought the market." While it is virtually impossible for an individual private investor to buy all 500 stocks in the S&P 500, it is easy to accomplish the same effect by buying shares in a mutual fund that replicates the index, such as the Vanguard 500 Index Fund (www.vanguard.com).

If you had invested $5,000 in the S&P 500 at the beginning of 1969 and then regularly added $5,000 each year for a total of $150,000, you would have amassed more than $2.5 million by the end of 1998. (See Figure 10.1.) Assume that dividends and other distributions were reinvested in additional shares. Automatic reinvestment of income and capital gains distributions is a simple thing when you buy shares of a mutual fund. Another helpful aspect of an index fund is that so long as you hold your shares, you will have very little capital gains taxes to pay because index funds employ a buy-and-hold strategy, which results in very little portfolio turnover and thus little realized capital gains.

FIGURE 10.1 / RESULTS OF $5,000 INVESTED IN A PORTFOLIO OF STOCKS REPLICATING THE S&P 500 ON JANUARY 2, 1969, PLUS $5,000 AT THE BEGINNING OF EACH YEAR TO DECEMBER 31, 1998.

YEAR	TOTAL RETURN	AMOUNT INVESTED	VALUE OF SHARES	ACCUMULATED AMOUNT INVESTED
1969	−8.4%	$5,000	$ 4,580	$ 5,000
1970	3.9	5,000	9,953	10,000
1971	14.2	5,000	17,077	15,000
1972	19.0	5,000	26,272	20,000
1973	−14.7	5,000	26,675	25,000
1974	−26.5	5,000	23,281	30,000
1975	37.2	5,000	38,801	35,000
1976	23.8	5,000	54,226	40,000
1977	−7.18	5,000	54,974	45,000
1978	6.5	5,000	63,908	50,000
1979	18.4	5,000	81,587	55,000
1980	32.4	5,000	114,641	60,000
1981	−4.91	5,000	113,755	65,000
1982	21.4	5,000	144,168	70,000
1983	22.5	5,000	182,731	75,000
1984	6.3	5,000	199,558	80,000
1985	32.2	5,000	270,426	85,000
1986	18.5	5,000	326,380	90,000
1987	5.2	5,000	348,711	95,000
1988	16.3	5,000	411,366	100,000
1989	31.5	5,000	547,522	105,000
1990	−3.2	5,000	534,840	110,000
1991	30.6	5,000	705,032	115,000
1992	7.7	5,000	764,704	120,000
1993	10.1	5,000	847,445	125,000
1994	1.3	5,000	863,526	130,000
1995	37.5	5,000	1,194,224	135,000
1996	22.9	5,000	1,473,846	140,000
1997	34.0	5,000	1,981,654	145,000
1998	28.6	$5,000	$2,554,837	$150,000

Beginning a Dollar Cost Averaging Program

How can you put dollar cost averaging to work for you? With mutual funds it's easy, thanks to a variety of automatic investment services that many fund families make available:

- *Bank transfer.* Under this plan, a fixed amount of money is electronically transferred from your bank account and invested in your mutual fund account on a regular basis. You set the amount (as little as $50) that can be invested monthly, bimonthly, quarterly, semiannually, or annually in the fund of your choice. You also can arrange for electronic transfer of funds on request.
- *Automatic exchange.* This service enables you to move money from one fund account to another regularly and automatically. You choose the date, the frequency, (monthly, bimonthly, quarterly, semiannually, or annually), and the amount (in dollars, shares, or a percentage of the current balance). Typically, shareholders exchange funds between a money market account and other funds whose share prices fluctuate.
- *Direct deposit.* This service provides an ideal way for you to deposit your paycheck or government payment, regardless of the frequency, into your mutual fund account.

Each service lets you set up an efficient and worry-free investment program because your money is transferred directly and automatically. IRA investors can take advantage of dollar cost averaging through the bank transfer and automatic exchange options. By establishing a regular investment schedule, you can contribute to your IRA automatically and through the convenience of easy monthly payments.

IN A NUTSHELL

Dollar cost averaging takes advantage of Wall Street's only certainty: the fluctuation of stock and bond prices. With dollar cost averaging, you are making the market's natural volatility work for you by lowering the average price you pay for your shares. Your average cost per share is always lower than the average price per share. There's no magic to it—just simple arithmetic.

Strategies to Minimize and Defer Taxes

Because your goal as an investor should be to keep as much as possible of what you earn from investments, you can't look past the inescapable reality that taxes take a big bite out of bottom-line returns. Investing in stocks, bonds, and mutual funds has many advantages, but beware of a potential hazard: The turnover of securities within your own or a mutual fund's portfolio often creates capital gains, the profits realized when the net cost of securities purchased is deducted from the net sale proceeds. A mutual fund must pass on these gains to all shareholders as taxable distributions, regardless of each investor's tax situation. For many investors, higher marginal federal income tax brackets as well as many states' taxes affect taxable dividends.

To help you develop a tax-efficient investment strategy, this chapter describes the impact of federal taxes on income and capital gains under the provisions of current tax law and then provides guidance on ways in which you can minimize your portfolio's exposure to taxes.

How Your Individually Owned Securities Are Taxed

Publicly held corporations will let you know whether their distributions are taxable. Taxable dividends paid to you are reported to the Internal Revenue Service (IRS) by the paying company on Form 1099-DIV, a copy of which is sent to you. Taxable interest paid to you is reported to the IRS by the payer on Form 1099-INT. The IRS uses this information as a check on your reporting of dividends and interest.

Cash Dividends

Cash dividends you receive that are paid out of current or accumulated earnings of a corporation are subject to tax as ordinary income.

Dividends Reinvested in Company Stock

Some companies allow you to take dividends in cash or reinvest the dividends in company stock. If you elect the stock plan and pay fair market value for the stock, the full cash dividend is taxable.

If the plan allows you to buy the stock at a discounted price, the amount of the taxable dividend is the fair market value of the stock on the dividend payment date less any service fee charged for the acquisition.

Stock Dividends and Stock Splits

If you own common stock and receive additional shares of the same company as a dividend, the dividend is generally not taxed, although preferred stock shareholders generally are taxed on stock dividends. A common stock dividend is taxed if the shareholder has the right to receive cash instead of stock or if the stock is that of another corporation.

Stock splits resemble the receipt of stock dividends, but they are not dividends. If you receive additional shares as part of a stock split, the new shares are not taxable. Even though you own more shares, your ownership percentage in the company has not changed.

Investment publications such as Moody's or Standard & Poor's annual dividend record books, available at many public libraries, provide details of dividend distributions and their tax treatment.

Real Estate Investment Trust (REIT) Dividends

Ordinary dividends from a REIT are fully taxable. Dividends designated by the trust as capital gains distributions are reported as long-term capital gains regardless of how long you have held your trust shares.

Return of Capital Distributions

A distribution that is not paid out of earnings is a nontaxable return of capital. It is, in effect, a partial payback of your investment. The distribution will be reported by the company on Form 1099-DIV as a nontaxable distribution.

Nontaxable distributions result in a reduction of the cost basis of your investment. If a return of capital distributions reduces your basis to zero, any further distributions are taxable as capital gains.

Money Market Fund Distributions

Distributions paid to you by money market funds are reportable as dividends. Don't confuse these with bank money market accounts, which pay interest, not dividends.

Interest on Corporate Bonds

Interest is taxable when received or made available to you.

Interest on U.S. Treasury Obligations

Interest on securities issued by the federal government is fully taxable on your federal return. However, interest on federal obligations is not subject to state or local income taxes. Interest on bonds and notes is taxable in the year received.

On a Treasury bill held to maturity, you report as interest the difference between the discounted price you paid and the amount you receive on redeeming the bill at maturity. If you dispose of the bill prior to maturity, taxable interest is the difference between the discounted price you paid and the proceeds you received.

Market Discount on Bonds

When the price of a bond declines because its interest rate is less than the current interest rate, a market discount occurs. Gain on a disposition of a bond bought after April 30, 1993, is taxable as ordinary income to the extent of the accrued market discount unless you reported it annually as interest income.

Original Issue Discount (OID) on Bonds

OID occurs when a bond is issued for a price less than its face or principal amount and is the difference between the principal amount and the issue price. All obligations that pay no interest before maturity, such as zero-coupon bonds, are considered to be issued at a discount. Normally, a portion of the OID must be reported as interest income each year you hold the bond.

Interest on State and Local Government Obligations

Normally, you pay no federal tax on the interest on bonds or notes of states, cities, counties, the District of Columbia, or a possession of the United States. However, interest on certain state and city obligations is taxable, such as federally guaranteed obligations and private activity bonds.

Most states tax the municipal bonds of other states but not their own. A few states and the District of Columbia don't tax the interest on any municipal obligations.

How Your Mutual Fund Investments Are Taxed

As an owner of mutual fund shares, you can be taxed two ways: on the earnings a fund makes while you own its shares and on profits you make when you sell or exchange shares. First I'll explain how a fund's earnings are taxed and then show how your sales or exchanges of shares may trigger taxes.

Owning Shares and Paying Taxes

A mutual fund is not taxed on the income of profits it earns on its investments as long as it passes those earnings along to shareholders. The shareholders, in turn, pay any taxes due. The two types of distributions that mutual funds make are income distributions and capital gains distributions:

1. *Income distributions* represent all interest and dividend income earned by a fund's securities—whether cash investments, bonds, or stocks—after subtracting the fund's operating expenses.
2. *Capital gains distributions* represent the profit a fund makes when it sells securities. When a fund makes such a profit, a capital gain is realized. When a fund sells securities at a price lower than it paid, it realizes a capital loss. If total capital gains exceed total capital losses, the fund has net-realized capital gains, which are distributed to fund shareholders. Net-realized capital

losses are not passed through to shareholders but are retained by the fund and may be used to offset future capital gains.

Occasionally, distributions from mutual funds may include a return of capital. Returns of capital are not taxed (unless they exceed your original cost basis) because they are considered a portion of your original investment being returned to you.

Generally, all income and capital gains distributions are subject to federal income taxes (and often state and local taxes as well). You must pay taxes on distributions regardless of whether you receive them in cash or reinvest them in additional shares. The exceptions to the general rule are:

- *U.S. Treasury securities,* whose interest income is exempt from state income taxes.
- *Municipal bond funds,* whose interest income is exempt from federal taxation and may be exempt from state taxation as well.

However, any capital gains on U.S. Treasury securities or municipal bond funds are generally taxable.

Although the amount of income and capital gains you receive from a mutual fund affects the taxes you pay, another important factor is the holding period for capital gains or losses—that is, how long the securities are held before they are sold or exchanged. Securities that are held for one year or less before they are sold or exchanged are categorized as short-term capital gains (or losses). Short-term capital gains are taxed at your ordinary rate. But long-term capital gains—gains on securities that are held for more than one year—are taxed at a maximum rate of 20 percent. (The long-term capital gains rate is 10 percent for taxpayers in the lowest income tax bracket.)

Your mutual fund will inform you of the category of any capital gains it distributes. The category is determined by how long the fund held the securities it sold, not by how long you have owned your shares of the fund. Income (such as interest and dividends) is taxed as ordinary income at your marginal tax.

IRS Form 1099-DIV, which your mutual fund usually sends in January for the previous tax year, details fund distributions you must report on your federal income tax return, including both income distributions and capital gains distributions. You won't receive a Form 1099-DIV for mutual funds on which you owe no taxes or for funds on which you earned less than $10 in dividends. (However, you still owe taxes on all fund distributions regardless of their size.)

Taxes on Sales or Exchanges of Shares

You can trigger taxes on mutual fund investments by selling some or all of your shares or by exchanging shares of one fund for shares of another. The length of time you hold shares and your tax bracket determine the tax rate on any gain.

Three important notes:

1. All capital gains from sales of mutual fund shares are taxable, even those from the sale of shares of a tax-exempt fund.
2. Exchanging shares between funds is considered a sale, which may lead to capital gains. (An exchange involves selling shares of one fund to buy shares in another.)
3. Writing a check against an investment in a mutual fund with a fluctuating share price (all funds except money market funds) also triggers a sale of shares and may expose you to tax on any resulting capital gains.

Strategies You Can Use to Minimize or Defer Taxes

Following are some simple techniques you can use to minimize the impact of taxes on your investment returns.

Time Your Investment Activities

Here's an example of how time may affect taxes on the sale of shares of an individual security or mutual fund: If you buy 100 shares of a security for $20 a share and sell them 6 months later for $22 a share, you owe taxes on your $200 short-term capital gain. If you're in the 31 percent marginal tax bracket, that's $62. However, if you hold on to the shares for more than 12 months after the original purchase, your profit is considered a long-term gain. Therefore, it is taxed at a maximum capital gains rate of 20 percent (for a maximum total tax of $40 on the $200 capital gain).

Emphasize Stocks with Low-Dividend Yields

If current income is not an important objective for you, invest in a diversified group of stocks that pay little or no dividends. Companies that choose to reinvest their earnings back into the company to finance future growth typically enable you to realize growth of your invested

---

FIGURE 11.1 / THE POWER OF LONG-TERM TAX DEFERRAL

**ANNUAL INVESTMENTS OF $1,000
(YEAR-END VALUES)**

NUMBER OF YEARS INVESTED	TAXABLE ACCOUNT	TAX-DEFERRED ACCOUNT BEFORE TAXES	TAX-DEFERRED ACCOUNT AFTER TAXES*
10	$13,477	$ 15,645	$13,782
15	23,361	29,324	24,597
20	36,194	49,423	39,713
25	52,854	78,954	61,149
30	$74,485	$122,346	$91,872

---

*Assumes an 8 percent annual rate of return and a 33 percent tax rate (federal and state combined).

capital together with deferred taxation (and ultimately pay taxes at the lower capital gains rate).

Make the Most of Tax-Deferred Accounts

Tax-deferred accounts, such as employer-sponsored retirement plans (401(k) and 403(b) plans), individual retirement accounts (traditional or Roth IRAs), or variable annuities, can have a dramatic impact on increasing your long-term investment returns. Figure 11.1 demonstrates the long-term benefit of delaying the payment of taxes. The Taxable Account column shows the value of annual $1,000 investments in a regular account on which taxes must be paid on the earnings every year. The Tax-Deferred Account Before Taxes column shows the value if the annual $1,000 investments are allowed to grow inside a tax-deferred account. The last column, Tax-Deferred Account After Taxes, shows the value of the tax-deferred account on the assumption that the account balance is withdrawn and taxes paid at the end of each period.

Though the advantage of tax deferral is evident early on, the difference becomes increasingly impressive over longer periods. The tax-deferred account grows to more than $122,000 after 30 years—nearly $48,000 more than the value of the taxable account over the same period. Even after taxes are paid at the end of the 30-year period, the tax-deferred account maintains an advantage of more than $17,000 over the taxable account—more than one-half the total investment of $30,000 over the 30-year period.

The benefit of tax deferral is even greater on investments that offer additional tax advantages, such as 401(k) or 403(b) accounts, which permit pretax contributions. For example, in a taxable account you would have to earn nearly $1,500 for every $1,000 of take-home pay that you plan to invest (assuming a 33 percent combined federal and state tax bracket). Therefore, by participating in a plan that allows pretax contributions, you could invest $1,500 without digging any deeper into your pocket than you would if you made a $1,000 investment after taxes.

The concept is similar for tax-deferred investments on which you may take a tax deduction, such as contributions to a traditional IRA. Receiving a tax deduction lightens the tax load by reducing the taxes that would otherwise be payable.

Usually people are not taxed on the earnings in tax-deferred accounts until they start withdrawing money from the accounts—typically during retirement. Whether the withdrawals take the form of a lump sum or an installment payment, the taxable portion is always considered ordinary income (as opposed to capital gains) and thus taxed at the taxpayer's marginal rate for the years when the withdrawals occur. (Note, however, that distributions from Roth IRAs after a taxpayer reaches age 59½ will be tax free if the Roth IRA has been held more than five years.)

Some tax-deferred investments offer added tax advantages. For example, you may be able to contribute wages or salary on a pretax basis. In a 401(k) plan, money you contribute to the plan is deducted from your pay before it is taxed, which reduces your taxable income. Similarly, many investors can deduct some or all of their contributions to traditional IRAs, which also reduces their taxable income. (Contributions to Roth IRAs are never deductible.)

Don't Buy a Tax Bill with Your Fund Shares

The tax owed on mutual fund investments also may depend in part on when you buy the shares. Mutual fund distributions, whether from income or capital gains, are taxed in the year they are made. Under certain circumstances, however, distributions declared during the last three months of a year and paid the following January are taxable in the year they were declared.

When a mutual fund (except for money market and bond funds) makes a distribution, its share price (or net asset value) falls by the amount of the distribution. For example, the net asset value of a mutual fund that trades for $20 a share ordinarily falls to $18 a share (not counting market activity) on the day its shareholders receive a $2 distribution. The impact on the value of your holdings is zero because you receive $2 in the distribution. However, you owe taxes on the entire $2 distribution.

As a result, when considering whether to purchase a fund, you need to know when the fund plans to make its next distribution. If you own shares of a fund on the fund's record date, you will receive a distribution. (Most mutual fund companies can tell you the projected timing and amount of upcoming distributions.) If you buy shares shortly before a distribution, you are simply "buying the dividend"—exposing yourself to taxes on the distribution but gaining no added value for the shares.

Seek Low Turnover

In your own portfolio or in a mutual fund, seek low turnover (the buying and selling of securities). Though most funds are not managed to keep taxes low, some types of mutual funds are tax friendly by nature, especially those that keep turnover low. A fund that buys and holds securities is likely to realize fewer taxable gains than a fund that engages in active trading—and thus less likely to pass along taxable gains to investors. You will enjoy the same tax-friendly result by employing a buy-and-hold strategy in your own portfolio.

Use Index Funds

The objective of an index fund is to match the performance and risk characteristics of a market benchmark, such as the Standard & Poor's 500-stock index. Stock index funds—but not bond index funds—can reduce an investor's exposure to taxes.

Index funds buy and hold the securities in a specific index (or a representative sample of the index). In this way, the portfolio turnover of index funds is typically low.

The chance that a security held in an index fund will be sold for a large gain (and thus generate a large tax bill for shareholders) is much lower than a fund that employs an active management approach (buying and selling securities at the fund manager's discretion).

Nonetheless, index funds do sometimes realize gains—for example, when a stock leaves a target index and must be sold by the fund. An index fund also could be forced to sell securities in its portfolio if many investors decide to sell their shares. (This can happen, for example, during a downturn in the stock market if many shareholders sell their mutual fund shares.)

Invest for Tax-Exempt Income

Interest on most municipal bonds is exempt from federal income taxes and, in some cases, from state and local income taxes as well. However, municipal bonds (or municipal bond funds) are not for everyone. Generally, investors in the 15 percent or 28 percent tax brackets do not benefit from owning municipal bonds.

Keep in mind that only a municipal bond's income is exempt from taxes. Taxes are payable on any capital gains that result from the sale of a municipal bond or fund. In addition, certain investors may be subject to the federal alternative minimum tax.

Use a Disciplined Sell-Selection Method

Finally, use such tax-minimizing techniques as selling securities in your portfolio with the highest original cost. In addition, when sensible, realize capital losses to help offset any realized capital gains.

IN A NUTSHELL

Investors typically concentrate on achieving maximum pretax returns. But you should develop a tax-efficient investment strategy to minimize your investment portfolio's exposure to taxes. What matters most is what's left over for you after taxes.

Investing in the Best Tax-Sheltered Retirement Plan for You

Americans have more options today than ever before when it comes to choosing the best way to save and invest for retirement. Thanks to the Taxpayer Relief Act of 1997—implemented in 1998— you now may choose from an array of individual retirement accounts (IRAs) that provide flexibility when planning for the day you say goodbye to the 9-to-5 grind.

Government-sponsored IRAs (traditional, Roth, Education, SIM-PLE, and SEP) and 401(k) plans provide two of the best ways to grow your fortune while taking advantage of important tax benefits. The trend in America today is for individuals to take responsibility for funding their own retirement needs. Increasing numbers of businesses are turning away from the pension plans that millions of workers traditionally counted on for retirement income and are asking workers to pay for and manage their own retirement plans.

The assets of 401(k) plans alone now surpass the $1 trillion mark. Money from all types of retirement plans is responsible for fueling much of the growth of the $5.5 trillion mutual fund industry. Mutual funds have been a good fit for participant-directed retirement plans because fund companies offer a broad investment choice to the average investor. They also convey information in a way the average investor can understand.

Traditional IRAs—a Popular Option

Traditional IRAs continue to be a very popular option for individual retirement plans. If you're under age 70½ and have earned income, you may be eligible to make tax-deductible contributions to a traditional IRA, but not, in general, if you participate in an employer-sponsored retirement plan, such as a 401(k) plan. In most cases, participation in such a plan means you don't qualify for a deductible IRA. However, if you meet certain adjusted gross income (AGI) requirements, you may still be able to take full or partial deductions regardless of your participation in an employer-sponsored plan. Fully deductible contributions may be possible if your AGI is below $30,000 (if you are single) or $50,000 (if you are married and file jointly). In addition, reduced deductible contributions may be allowed for AGI levels between $30,000 to $40,000 (single) and $50,000 to $60,000 (married couples filing jointly).

If you're a qualified individual, you're allowed to contribute and deduct the full $2,000 (or 100 percent of your earned income, whichever is less) annually until age 70½, at which time you are required to begin taking distributions from the plan. Married couples filing jointly are allowed to contribute and deduct $4,000 per year.

Not only are your contributions tax deductible, but your earnings also will grow tax deferred until withdrawal, at which time they are taxed as ordinary income. As long as those withdrawals are made after age 59½ (earlier if used to buy a first home, for higher education expenses, or on your death), there is no 10 percent early withdrawal penalty.

If you participate in an employer-sponsored plan and your AGI won't qualify you to make deductible contributions, you are still eligible to make nondeductible contributions to a traditional IRA as long as you are under age 70½ and have earned income. These after-tax contributions are subject to the same restrictions as their deductible counterparts and, like the deductible plans, earnings also grow tax deferred. These contributions may be recovered tax free when distributions are made. Again, if withdrawals are made after age 59½ (earlier if used to buy your first home, to pay higher education expenses, or on your death), there is no 10 percent early withdrawal penalty. Nondeductible contributions must be designated on Form 8606 and attached to Form 1040 for the year of contribution.

Roth IRAs—Tax-Free Buildup and Withdrawal

Roth IRAs arrived on the financial scene in January 1998. Although contributions to Roth IRAs are not deductible, these plans provide one key benefit: Once your after-tax contributions have been in a Roth IRA for at least five years—and if you are 59½ or older (earlier if you are buying your first home)—you can make withdrawals tax free and penalty free.

Thus, Roth IRAs give you the tax advantage at the time of distribution instead of at the time of contribution, as is the case with traditional IRAs. An important aspect of this difference is that the earnings (i.e., interest, dividends, or capital gains) are not just tax deferred as with a traditional IRA; they may be withdrawn tax free along with the contributions. Also, there is no requirement to take distributions when you turn 70½, and if you have earned income after 70½, you can contribute to your Roth IRA as long as you like.

Roth IRAs do have eligibility guidelines, and qualified individuals may contribute $2,000 ($4,000 if married and filing jointly) annually, not counting rollover contributions. If your AGI is less than or equal to $95,000, or if you and your spouse are filing jointly with an AGI less than or equal to $150,000, you are eligible to make full contributions to a Roth IRA. Your total IRA contributions (Roth and traditional) may not exceed $2,000 per year, per person.

If your AGI is between $95,000 and $110,000, or if you and your spouse are filing jointly with an AGI between $150,000 and $160,000, your eligibility will be phased out. If your AGI is greater than $110,000, or if you and your spouse file jointly and have an AGI greater than $160,000, you are not eligible to make contributions to a Roth IRA.

Many individuals have converted their traditional IRAs to Roth IRAs to take advantage of the tax-free buildup and withdrawals. If your AGI is $100,000 or less, you may roll over your account—subject to ordinary income taxation at the time of rollover—from a traditional IRA to a Roth IRA without an early withdrawal penalty.

It is important to remember that rolling money over from a traditional IRA to a Roth IRA means you must first pay taxes on money in your traditional IRA that was not previously taxed. If your contributions were tax deductible, you must pay taxes on the whole amount, whereas if you made nondeductible contributions, you are taxed on your earnings only.

If you're trying to decide between making a new contribution to a traditional IRA or a Roth IRA, you may want to talk with your financial adviser or tax accountant to determine whether the tax advantages are more beneficial for you at the time of contribution or on withdrawal down the road. Working with a professional who has your best interest in mind (and not a possible commission) will help ensure that you are making the right decision.

Education IRAs

Education IRAs are not really retirement accounts at all. They are education accounts with characteristics similar to those of Roth IRAs; the money contributed to Education IRAs is not deductible but is, along with earnings, not taxed when withdrawn. Education IRAs also allow for tax-free, penalty-free distributions if the money is used for your beneficiaries' qualified higher education expenses (tuition, fees, books, supplies, or room and board at an eligible institution).

You are eligible to make contributions to an Education IRA only if your AGI is less than $95,000 (less than $150,000 for married couples filing jointly). You may establish these accounts as trust or custodial accounts for children or grandchildren age 18 or younger. Annual nondeductible contributions are limited to $500 per beneficiary.

SIMPLE and SEP IRAs

Employees of small businesses and self-employed individuals may be eligible for two excellent options for retirement savings—SIMPLE (Savings Incentive Match Plan for Employees) and SEP (simplified employee pension) IRAs.

The SIMPLE IRA applies to employers with no more than 100 employees who have received compensation of $5,000 or more during the preceding calendar year. To qualify, employers cannot maintain another qualified plan for employees. Employers must either match the employee's elective contributions (dollar-for-dollar up to 3 percent—but not less than 1 percent for any two years within a rolling five-year period—of the employee's compensation) or make a 2 percent nonelective contribution for each eligible employee. Under this second option, employers must make a contribution to a SIMPLE IRA for each employee who is eligible to participate, regardless of whether a particular employee makes any contributions on his or her own behalf.

Employees may make up to $6,000 per year in employee salary reduction contributions, and employees are 100 percent vested immediately on making a contribution. As with any other retirement plan, a variety of restrictions apply to distributions taken from the plan, so check with your financial adviser for more information.

SEP IRAs don't require a specific number of employees—or a specific employee salary level—for employers to qualify. Employer contributions are discretionary and may be as high as 15 percent of an employee's salary or $24,000, whichever is less.

A notable feature of both the SIMPLE and the SEP IRA is that they allow employees to contribute up to $2,000 to a traditional or Roth IRA in addition to SIMPLE or SEP contributions.

401(k) Plans

You may be eligible for a 401(k) plan, now available to employees of large and medium-sized companies, and an increasing number of small companies. In many major corporations, pension plans are rapidly being overtaken by these plans, which require employees to put in their own money for retirement and make their own decisions on how the funds will be invested. Thus, an employee may elect to reduce his or her taxable compensation with contributions to a 401(k) plan where those amounts will accumulate tax free. Employers often match these amounts with employer contributions. Employees of nonprofit organizations may be eligible for a similar 403(b) plan.

Named after a section of the Internal Revenue Code that authorizes it, 401(k) plans have been available since 1978. Under such plans, employees put a percentage of their pretax earnings into an investment account, where the money grows free of taxation until the employees' retirement. Most 401(k) plans offer a selection of investment options, usually mutual funds. Expanding from the three or four funds that used to be standard, employees now often can choose from among one dozen, two dozen, or more mutual funds. Some employers also have begun to embrace a radically different option even if it can be risky for many workers. It is a self-managed 401(k) account that lets an employee choose from thousands of stocks, bonds, and mutual funds while still able to invest in the plan's other choices.

At an employee's retirement, the 401(k) plan provides one lump-sum distribution, the size of which depends on how much the employee saved during the years and how effectively it was invested. Like other retirement plans, assets may be rolled over or transferred to an IRA.

Yet many participants are not setting aside enough money in their 401(k) plans and they are poorly investing what they do save. In addition, participating employees frequently turn to these retirement accounts for cash to cover everything from houses to cars to medical bills. Remember, a successful retirement plan requires a long-term commitment to savings.

IN A NUTSHELL

IRAs and 401(k) plans offered by employers represent two excellent vehicles for building your retirement funds on a highly tax-favored basis. Although not all wage earners qualify for tax-deductible IRA contributions, nearly all can take advantage of the tax-deferred accumulation privilege. So begin early and contribute generously.

Intelligent Investing

The extraordinary volatility in the financial markets is just one example of the stepped-up pace of our lives in a new era in which the technology revolution, the information explosion, and the rise of global interdependence have altered almost every activity in our daily life. To a large extent, these developments have brought the citizens of the United States unprecedented prosperity and accumulation of wealth. Investors now have all the information they need—except, of course, information about the future course of events and markets—to make investment decisions. But information should not be mistaken for wisdom, the ultimate weapon of the intelligent investor.

To earn the highest returns that are *realistically* possible, you should invest with simplicity. Rely on the ordinary virtues that intelligent people have relied on for centuries: common sense, thrift, realistic expectations, patience, and perseverance. If you hold to these values, over the long run your investing will be rewarded.

The great paradox of the remarkable age in which we live is that the more complex the world around us becomes, the more simplicity we must seek to realize our financial goals. Don't underrate simplicity or its proven effectiveness as a long-term strategy for productive investing. Simplicity is the master key to financial success.

Fundamental Investment Principles

Given the recent volatility we have witnessed in the financial markets, it is worthwhile to reaffirm four fundamental investment principles:

1. *Balance.* The simple idea that investors should balance their stock holdings with bond holdings.
2. *Markets fluctuate.* Too many investors think stocks provide a one-way ticket to the accumulation of wealth.
3. *Invest for the long term.* When sharp market drops occur, too many investors, focused on the short term, sell or cease buying.
4. *Stay the course.* No matter what the markets give us, common stocks should remain the principal asset class in a long-term investment program.

A Simple Rule for Investment Success

Simplicity gives us a surprising rule for measuring investment success. The central task of investing is to realize the highest possible portion of the return earned in the financial class in which you invest—realizing, and accepting, that that portion will be less than 100 percent.

Why? Because of cost. We know intuitively that our cash reserves will inevitably earn less than the going market rate for short-term commercial paper. Our certificates of deposit and money market funds will yield less simply because the costs of financial intermediaries—transaction costs, information costs, and the cost of convenience—will be deducted from the interest rates paid by the government or corporate borrower.

Similarly, we don't expect bond mutual funds to provide us with higher yields than the average yield of the bonds held in a fund's portfolio. In fact, because of excessive fees in bond funds as a group, the gap between 100 percent of the market return and the return that filters down to the investor after cost is often distressingly large—so large that most bond funds turn out to be distinctly inferior investments.

Even in the equity arena, it is simply a mathematical impossibility for all investors as a group to reach 100 percent of the stock market's returns. Given the excessive costs of most equity mutual funds, it is a mathematical certainty that over a lifetime of investing only a relative handful of investors can succeed in doing so by any significant margin. Accepting this reality—that investors as a group will inevitably capture less than 100 percent of the rate of return provided in any asset class—is the first step in simplifying our investment decisions.

Investing in a Single Balanced Index Fund

Consider that the ultimate in simplicity comes with the additional virtue of low cost. The simplest of all approaches is to invest in a single balanced market index fund only—just one fund (such as the Vanguard Balanced Index Fund [www.vanguard.com]). And it works. Such a fund offers a broadly diversified middle-of-the-road investment program for a typical conservative investor, allocating about 65 percent of assets to stocks and 35 percent to bonds. Over the past 15 years, it would have captured 99 percent of the rate of return of the combined stock and bond markets. An index fund attempts to replicate the investment results of a target index by holding all, or a representative sample of, the securities in the index. (See Chapter 28 for more on index funds.)

It is illuminating to compare the cumulative returns of actively managed balanced mutual funds—a group whose portfolios tend to be quite homogeneous—with the cumulative returns of a no-load balanced index fund weighted 35 percent by the total U.S. bond market (the Lehman Brothers Aggregate Bond index) and 65 percent by the total U.S. stock market (the Wilshire 5000 Equity index) with the annual return reduced by estimated costs of 0.2 percent. The results in June 1998 for a $10,000 investment made in June 1983 show that the final value of the average actively managed balanced fund was $60,900 versus a final value of $76,200 for an index balanced fund. Actively managed balanced funds had an average annual total return of 12.8 percent and achieved 87 percent of the market return. The index balanced fund achieved 99 percent of the market return with a 14.5 percent average annual total return.

What accounts for the superiority of the index fund? Not magic, but costs. The heavy costs of the managed funds were primarily responsible for their shortfall. The average balanced fund incurred annual operating expenses of 1.1 percent during the period, and perhaps another 0.4 percent in portfolio turnover costs, a total handicap of 1.5 percent. The index fund total cost was 0.2 percent, an advantage of 1.3 percent that accounted for most of the difference in return. To make matters worse, because of recently increased mutual fund costs, the average total cost of a balanced fund today is about 2.2 percent, almost

50 percent higher than the past average, giving the index fund an even greater advantage in the future.

Today there are nearly 400 balanced funds to choose from, a reflection both on the broad acceptance of the principle of balance and the explosive growth of the mutual fund industry. Implementing an investment program with a single balanced index fund is obviously the ultimate in simplicity.

Investing in a Single Stock Index Fund

A second example of the value of simplicity for your stock portfolio is a single equity index fund. Again, during the past 15 years the past record of indexing has been truly remarkable. The results in June 1998 for a $10,000 investment made in June 1983 show that the final value of the average actively managed diversified equity fund was $66,800 versus a final value of $90,300 for a total stock market index fund. The total stock market index (again, the Wilshire 5000) outpaced the average diversified equity fund by 2.3 percentage points per year. And again the 15.8 percent average annual total return of the index fund captured 99 percent of the market's annual return of 16 percent. The managed equity funds captured just 84 percent, with an average annual total return of just 13.5 percent. The added return on a $10,000 investment was $23,500, some two and one-half times the entire value of the initial investment. This 2.3 percent difference arises largely because the total costs of the managed funds averaged about two full percentage points.

Someone might say: "The index fund is always fully invested in stocks, so why not hire a manager who can reduce stock holdings in anticipation of market declines?" This sounds like a good strategy, but it fails in practice. In fact, fund managers have done exactly the reverse. For example, equity funds as a group held an average cash position equal to 12 percent of assets at the start of the great bull market that started in the early 1970s. Near the market high in July 1998, fund cash had been cut to only 5 percent of assets, providing little protection against the decline that ensued. Being bearish when you should be bullish and bullish when you should be bearish is not a formula for success. In fact, it is impossible to correctly predict the future course of the stock market with any consistency.

In addition, equity funds tend to hold riskier stocks than the overall market, leaning toward more volatile growth issues and small cap stocks. An all-market index fund has been about 20 percent less volatile than the average managed fund. In the 20 percent market decline that occurred in 1998, the average managed fund declined by more than 22 percent.

The indexing investment strategy discussed above is the very essence of simplicity: owning the entire U.S. stock market (and for balanced funds the entire U.S. bond market); making no effort to select the best manager; holding the asset allocation fairly constant and refusing to consider market timing; keeping transaction activity low, minimizing taxes; and eliminating the excessive costs of investing that characterize most mutual funds. And it works!

Nonindexing Rules for Intelligent Investing

In spite of the discussion above, many investors choose to pursue the conventional strategy of relying entirely on actively managing their own investments or utilizing actively managed mutual funds. In the real world, lots of all-too-human traits get in the way of a simple, all-encompassing index fund approach. All too common refrains include: "I'm better than average"; "Even if the game is expensive, it's fun"; and "It can't be that simple."

After all, in a given ten-year period, about one of every five actively managed mutual funds has outpaced the market (after taxes, one of seven). If these are not great odds in the investor's favor, however, they are not insurmountable. And there are some simple commonsense principles that should help you invest or select funds that can earn a generous portion of the market's return. If there are long odds against outpacing the market, at least going about the task intelligently can help to ensure against a significant failure. Following are some rules that will help you avoid common problems.

Keep Costs Low

Costs matter. The average equity mutual fund now charges 1.54 percent in expenses, and portfolio transaction costs can bring the total annual expenses to 2 percent or more. This is likely to cut the returns their investors earn by 20 percent or more over time. The total costs for bond funds average 1.2 percent. Such costs would cut today's yield of 5.2 percent on the 30-year U.S. Treasury bond to 4 percent, or by fully 23 percent.

A low expense ratio is the single most important reason why an investment portfolio does well. Lower costs are the handmaiden of higher returns. Today's average fund portfolio turnover of 85 percent a year carries transaction costs that reduce returns by as much as 0.5 to 1 percentage points over and above the cost of fund expenses. Plus it carries enormous tax costs. If your portfolio or fund holdings are in taxable accounts (i.e., other than in a tax-deferred IRA or a 401(k) plan), high turnover can not only cause you to pay full income taxes on short-term gains but also deprive you of the extraordinary value of the deferral of capital gains taxes. Never forget that taxes are costs too.

Consider Carefully the Added Costs of Advice

Millions of investors need personal assistance and guidance in allocating their assets and selecting securities. Other millions do not. If you are in the latter category, you can invest online and choose from among some 6,000 stocks and 3,000 no-load mutual funds; it is the essence of simplicity for the self-reliant, intelligent, informed investor to purchase shares without an intermediary salesperson or financial adviser.

For the many who require guidance, good advisers give you their personal attention, help you avoid some of the pitfalls of investing, and provide worthwhile asset allocation and security selection services. But like any of us, they must earn their keep, providing services of sufficient value to you to make it worth your while to retain them. You should know exactly how much their services will cost. Figure 13.1 illustrates some of the added costs of advice.

FIGURE 13.1 / THE ADDED COSTS OF ADVICE

		TYPICAL ANNUAL COST
Investment Advisers		1%
Stock brokers	Commissions	4
	Front-end loads	6*
	Spread loads	1
Hidden loads	12b-1 fees	1
Funds of funds and wrap accounts		1–2

---

*First year only

Don't Overrate Past Performance

Track records are usually hopelessly misleading in appraising how money managers or mutual funds will perform in the future. There is simply no way to forecast future returns based on a manager's past record. Studies show, however, that managers with past returns that have been substantially superior to the returns of an appropriate market index will regress toward, and usually below, the market mean over time. For example, in two studies of returns over consecutive decades, 99 percent of top-quartile mutual funds moved closer to—and even below—the market mean from the first ten-year period to the subsequent ten-year period. The only exception was a fund that was superior during the 1970s and 1980s alike; but so far in the 1990s, it has regressed, falling far below the market's return.

The record is clear that top-performing funds inevitably lose their edge. Yet fund sponsors persist in promoting their most successful (past) performers. Such a strategy defies reason except that promotion of such funds brings in lots of new money and lots of new fees to the adviser. But such promotions lead investors in precisely the wrong direction. Ignore them.

Use Past Performance to Determine Consistency

There *is* an important role that past performance can play in helping you make your fund or manager selections. Even though you should disregard a single aggregate number showing past long-term return, you can learn a great deal by studying the nature of past returns. Look for consistency. Look at the ranking of a portfolio manager or fund compared with the manager's or the fund's peers (those with similar policies and objectives). Thus, compare a large cap fund with other large cap funds, a small cap fund with comparable funds, and so on.

Beware of Stars

Portfolio managers who rise to star status have been few and are hardly ever identified in advance. Who ever heard of Peter Lynch or Michael Price in 1972, at the beginning of the bull market, before their excellent records were achieved? To make matters worse, even the superstars seem to have a limited longevity with a given fund. The average portfolio manager lasts just five years at the helm. When a new manager takes over, the result is high portfolio turnover, which is costly and tax inefficient. Seek good managers, but rely on workmanlike professionalism, experience, and steadfastness rather than stardom.

Beware of Too-Big Asset Size

Funds can get too big. It's as simple as that. Avoid large funds that have no history of closing funds to new investors and those that seem willing to let their funds grow to seemingly infinite size beyond their power to differentiate their investment results from the crowd and irrespective of their investment goals.

Deciding what is too big is complex. It relates to fund style, fund management philosophy, and fund portfolio strategy. A giant fund—say $20 billion—investing in large cap stocks with very little portfolio turnover can be managed effectively, though not for truly exceptional returns. For a fund investing aggressively in microcap stocks, $300 million might be too large.

The record shows that for the overwhelming majority of funds, their best years came when they were small. When funds catch the public fancy—and are vigorously sold to a public unsuspecting of their potential exposure to the problems of size—their best years are behind them. Unbridled growth should be a warning to any intelligent investor.

Don't Own Too Many Funds

How many funds should you own? If a single ready-made 65 percent stock/35 percent bond index fund can meet the needs of many investors, and if a pair of stock and bond index funds with a custom-made balance can meet the needs of many more, what is the optimal number of funds for investors who elect to use actively managed funds? Probably no more than four or five equity funds and one or at most two bond funds. Owning too many stock funds can easily result in a dangerous combination of overdiversification and excessive cost.

Buy Your Portfolio—and Hold It

Once you've decided on your long-term objectives, define your tolerance for risk and carefully select a diversified portfolio of securities or a small number of mutual funds. Then follow this last rule: Hold tight. Stay the course. Complicating the investment process merely clutters the mind, too often bringing emotion into a financial plan that cries out for rationality. Investor emotions such as hope, greed, and fear—if translated into rash actions—can be every bit as destructive to investment performance as inferior market returns. Warren Buffett, as successful as investors get, once said: "Inactivity strikes us as intelligent behavior."

The key to holding tight is buying right. Buying right is picking securities or funds you understand. It is not buying shares on the basis of past performance; it is not picking stocks or funds because someone tells you they are hot; it is not buying shares of high-cost funds. If you avoid these fundamental errors, simply keep an eye on your securities' performance and patiently tolerate periodic declines. If it's wise to "investigate before you invest," it's equally wise to "investigate before you divest."

IN A NUTSHELL

To earn the highest returns on your long-term investments, invest with simplicity. Rely on the common virtues that intelligent people have relied on for centuries: common sense, thrift, realistic expectations, patience, and perseverance.

Matching Your Existing Portfolio to Your Goals

If you already have a portfolio of investments, now is an opportune time to take stock, look ahead, and make sure your investments are appropriate for your long-term financial goals. This chapter will help you organize your existing holdings by category: stability, income, or growth. Next, you can estimate the amount of money you will need in the future to achieve your major goals. You then can compare these categories to see if what you have matches what you'll need. As a last step, you can identify one or more strategies to help you align your portfolio with your goals.

You may find you want to obtain new investments to fill any gaps or to compensate for shortfalls. Perhaps your portfolio is heavy in short-term or conservative investments relative to your needs and light on those for long-term growth. And if you have more assets than necessary for a particular goal, you may want to reallocate some to other areas.

Take a Look at Where You Are

The first step in your financial review—a step often overlooked—is to make a list of your current investments and classify each by its main objective—stability, income, or growth. As you classify your investments, ask yourself: Is this investment intended to provide stability of principal? Does it provide income or perhaps income and some growth? Or do I own it solely for its potential to provide capital appreciation (growth) over time and to protect my assets against inflation?

FIGURE 14.1 / INVESTMENTS AND THEIR CHARACTERISTICS

CATEGORY	STABILITY CASH RESERVES	INCOME 3–5 YEARS	GROWTH OVER 5 YEARS
Typical investments	Money market funds	Short-term and intermediate-term bonds, bond funds	U.S. and foreign stocks and stock funds
	CDs or bank deposits		
		Most conservative stock funds for goals at least 5 years distant	
Investment characteristics	Your most conservative investments—price that doesn't change at all	Conservative and moderately aggressive investments—high-income potential	More aggressive investments—history of high returns over time; often little or no income
	Easy access to money; regular income payments	Regular income payments	Returns that consistently outpace inflation

---

For example, your investments that provide stability, such as bank CDs and money market funds, supply the liquidity you need for your near-term goals and for an ongoing reserve for contingencies.

Your investments that provide income and perhaps some growth include bonds, bond funds, and your most conservative income-oriented stocks or stock funds. These investments are usually appropriate for intermediate-term goals three to five years away.

Your stocks or stock funds, many of which generate little or no income, are your growth investments. You are counting on these to provide the capital you'll need in six or more years, perhaps for your children's college expenses or for your retirement nest egg.

Figure 14.1 provides examples of investment types and how they fit into the categories of stability, income, and growth. After you complete your list, calculate totals for each category—stability, income, growth—and also a grand total. Then jot down the percentage each category represents of your total investments (divide each category total by the grand total).

Focus on Your Financial Goals

Give some thought to your financial goals so you can perform a reality check on your portfolio holdings. How much money will you need to meet these goals? Aim for ballpark figures. Write down specific goals and the amount of money needed.

- *Cash reserves:* The rule of thumb is that your cash reserves should equal three to six months of living expenses, but you may want more if you face a large expenditure in the near future, such as a tuition bill, tax payment, or wedding.
- *Intermediate-term goals:* Important objectives that are three to five years away also could include education expenses or perhaps a down payment on a home.
- *Longer-term goals:* The most universal longer-term goal is retirement. Experts typically say you will need 60 to 80 percent of your income level at retirement to maintain your living standard. According to the Social Security Administration, Social Security may supply about 21 percent of your needed retirement income, and you also may be entitled to a pension. Increasingly, however, it is clear that you will need to supplement these sources to live comfortably in retirement.

Align Your Portfolio with Your Goals

What if your holdings don't reflect your financial goals? Perhaps you have too large a percentage of your money in stable investments and not enough going into growth investments for your retirement fund. Or perhaps you overlooked the intermediate area—money that needs to be conservatively invested for a goal not more than five years away.

If your current holdings don't line up with your longer-term needs, you may want to adjust them now or incrementally over time. If your investments do line up with your future needs, you still need to decide where to invest additional money over the coming months. You

FIGURE 14.2 / SAMPLE STRATEGIES FOR LONGER-TERM GOALS

	RISK-RETURN PORTFOLIOS		
	LOWER RISK	MODERATE RISK	HIGHER RISK
Money markets	20.0%	10.0%	0.0%
Bonds	40.0	30.0	20.0
Stocks	40.0	60.0	80.0
Average annual return: 1995–1997	8.8%	9.9%	10.8%

may want to maintain your current allocations or you might need to fine-tune them to compensate for market movements.

To help you with decisions for longer-term goals, Figure 14.2 illustrates three basic portfolios—three combinations of investments representing stability, income, and growth—to provide a useful frame of reference. Each portfolio has a distinct potential risk-reward profile—lower, moderate, higher—and for each I have included some historical data to show you how it would have performed in the past, using major indexes to represent the major asset classes.

Strategies to Consider

Think about your time horizon for your financial goals and carefully consider the amount of risk you believe you are comfortable with. Remember, for near-term goals you should assume little or no risk. Consider these strategies:

- Sell assets in the surplus areas of your portfolio and reinvest the proceeds in the deficit areas. Keep in mind that this may result in taxable gains.
- Exchange assets among mutual funds managed by a single company. This also may result in taxable gains.
- Make a new, lump-sum investment in your deficit area.
- Set up a systematic investing program in which securities are purchased automatically from your paycheck, bank account, or a money market fund.

FIGURE 14.3 / THE POWER OF COMPOUNDING

MONTHLY INVESTMENT	PRETAX AMOUNTS YOU CAN ACCUMULATE OVER TIME			
	5 YEARS	**10 YEARS**	**20 YEARS**	**30 YEARS**
$ 50	$ 3,698	$ 9,208	$ 29,647	$ 75,015
100	7,397	18,417	59,295	150,037
200	14,793	36,833	118,589	300,059
500	36,983	92,083	296,474	750,148

To help you estimate how much you might need to save systematically for building the future capital you need, review Figure 14.3. It shows how various amounts invested monthly would grow over 5, 10, 20, or 30 years, assuming an 8 percent annual rate of return compounded monthly. Find the amounts that approximate those you need for your various goals, and then decide how much you might want to invest monthly to achieve them.

If maintained over a period of time, a systematic program allows dollar cost averaging—purchasing more shares at lower prices and vice versa. (This does not ensure a profit or protect against a loss in declining markets.) See Chapter 10 for more on dollar cost averaging.

IN A NUTSHELL

It makes sense from time to time to take stock, look ahead, and make sure your investments continue to be appropriate for your long-term financial goals. Perhaps the risk-reward composition of your portfolio no longer matches your needs. You may want to direct new investments to fill any gaps or to compensate for a shortfall, and you may want to reallocate some assets to other areas.

Investing in Stocks

Realistic Expectations for Stock Market Returns

According to the American Association of Individual Investors, if at the end of 1940 you had invested $1,000 in the stocks of the Standard & Poor's 500 index (S&P 500), you would now have more than $1 million (reinvesting dividends and excluding taxes).

If you had invested the same $1,000 in small company stocks, you would now have more than $6 million! Shares of these smaller companies generally have been purchased by individuals, showing that you, as an individual, can outperform the institutions and the popular market averages.

Is Timing Important?

Many individuals hesitate to invest in stocks on any given day. "The market is too high," they say. The stock market goes up about two out of three days. With such friendly odds, you risk more by being out of the market than being in it! In fact, every day you wait could cost you money. It doesn't pay to wait for the right time to get in on a market dip. It isn't particularly important what level the market is at when you start investing. Even an investor with the most pathetic luck imaginable does just fine if he or she keeps at it, as illustrated by the mythical Warren and his brother-in-law Harry.

It all starts back in the early 1960s with Warren, the single unluckiest investor in the entire world. Starting in 1963, he put $2,000 once a year into the stocks that comprise the S&P 500 index—but his timing was so terrible that he chose the worst day of the year every time! Incredibly, he invested at the exact top of the market every year—and kept it up for ten years. (After that, he let it ride.)

As of the end of 1998, his total of $20,000 would have grown to $716,144.

But Warren's brother-in-law Harry started investing $2,000 a year in 1973, right after Warren quit. To everyone's astonishment, especially Warren's, Harry turned out to be the world's luckiest investor. Every year he picked the absolute bottom of the market to plunk down his $2,000. And to stack the odds in Harry's favor even more, he kept up this stupendous performance for 20 years, investing twice as much and twice as long as Warren.

Guess what: As of the end of 1998, Harry's $40,000 investment would be worth $22,144 *less* than Warren's stake—$694,000 versus $716,144. Imagine! Harry put in twice the money and his annual return was far higher, yet Warren beat him easily. Moral: Forget market timing. Timing and luck are nice, but you can make more money by just getting started now. Say you had invested for 30 years in the S&P 500 at the start of every year since 1965. As of mid-1995, you would have racked up an annual return of 11 percent. But what if you were unlucky enough to have invested at the high of the market each year? It would hardly have mattered. Your annualized return would have been reduced only to 10.6 percent.

Conversely, if you had had the good fortune to invest at the bottom of the market each year, your return would have risen only 0.7 percent to 11.7 percent. In other words, it doesn't matter much in the long run whether your timing is great or terrible. What matters is that you *stay invested.* It's time—not timing—that is going to make you rich.

The past couple of decades have been nothing short of spectacular for the U.S. stock market. As you consider your investment strategies, it's understandable that you might focus on the reward half of the risk-reward equation. Stock prices soared to record after record, carrying stock valuations above historical norms in relation to dividends, book value, and earnings. As a prudent investor, however, it is especially important to consider the other half of the equation: the risk of investing in common stocks.

Expect Volatility in the Stock Market

Among all financial assets, equities have proven to be the most effective for long-term capital growth. They also, however, involve more risk than do many other types of investments. Over the long term, returns provided by common stocks have averaged 11 percent annually. But this average return conceals a great deal of volatility. Returns from stocks have fluctuated within a very wide band. Since 1926, the stock market has provided annual returns ranging from a low of –43.3 percent (in 1931) to a high of +53.9 percent (in 1933), as noted earlier.

This extreme volatility is the chief risk you face when investing in common stocks. But it is a risk that is often overlooked after the recent lengthy period of generally rising stock prices. The bear markets of 1987, 1990, and 1998 were unusually short, the ones in 1987 and 1998 being over so quickly that there were actually positive returns for those years. It's easy for new investors to underestimate the volatility of common stocks because volatility has been muted in the past two decades. Until 1998, the stock market as a whole had not suffered a price decline, from high to low, of more than 10 percent since late 1990, making that the longest period ever without such a decline. In 1998, despite the short-lived market retreat (down 12.6 percent from July to September), the market managed a gain for the full year.

Longer holding periods of stock mitigate, but do not eliminate, the volatility in returns from common stocks. As the holding period for stocks increases, the bands within which fluctuations occur narrows. For instance, over 5-year periods beginning in 1926 and ending in 1997, average annual returns on stocks ranged from –12.5 percent to +23.9 percent. Over 10-year periods, the range of average annual returns has been narrower, from –0.9 percent to +20.1 percent. Over 20-year holding periods, average annual returns ranged from +3.1 percent to +16.9 percent.

What lessons can we learn from these statistics? First, time reduces the risks of holding common stocks. This is important to keep in mind when developing your investment strategy. Think long term. Second, there is no guarantee that you will earn the long-term average return of 11 percent a year, even if you hold stocks for 20 years or more. Third, the 4 years from 1995 through 1998, when the S&P 500 provided total annual returns of 37.6 percent, 22.9 percent, 33.9 percent, and 28.6 percent, respectively, may already have provided a large part of the returns that can reasonably be expected over the next several years.

Expect Bear Markets

If you are relatively new to investing in common stocks, take a moment to review some bear markets. Incidentally, a bear market refers to a prolonged period of falling prices. No general agreement

exists about how steeply or for how long prices must decline to consti-
tute a bear market (some observers assert that prices must fall at least
20 percent to qualify). Over the past 40 years, 9 downturns could have
been described as bear markets, with prices declining 20 percent or
more from their highs. The shortest of these lasted just 3 months and
the longest nearly 3 years.

Historically, the S&P 500 has declined an average of 28 percent
during bear markets. The worst of the post–World War II bear markets
occurred during the period from January 10, 1973, until December 6,
1974. This 23-month bear market resulted in a loss to shareholders of
48 percent of the market's value. It was not until 1982 that the market
returned to its level of January 1973.

No one can consistently predict the timing of market declines.
Bear markets can and will occur from time to time. So you should
understand the extent to which prices can drop and be prepared to ride
out, and even take advantage of, these market retreats to buy more
shares when prices are low. The worst danger you face from bear markets is that you will sell at or near the bottom of a downturn. Many
investors did just that during the severe bear market of 1973 to 1974,
missing out on an extraordinary rebound in stock market performance.
During the 10 years from 1975 to 1984, the S&P 500 produced an average annual return of 14.8 percent. From 1975 to 1989, the annual return
averaged 16.6 percent and for the 20-year period beginning in 1975,
the return averaged 14.6 percent. The long-term winners were investors who persevered. They took advantage of lower prices to add to
their portfolios.

Expect Reasonable Returns

Investment returns are unpredictable over the short term, even
over a term of several years. This is one reason why investors rely so
much on long-term historical averages in setting their expectations
about future returns. John C. Bogle, senior chairman of The Vanguard
Group, says three components are needed for forecasting returns from
common stocks: the dividend yield, the rate of growth in earnings, and
the impact on total return from changes in the initial price-earnings
multiple for stocks.

In early 1999, the dividend yield on the S&P 500 was 1.34 percent, well below the historical average of about 4 percent. For the other
components, you might assume that they will revert toward their long-

term historical averages. Over the past 30 years, the growth rate for corporate earnings of the largest 500 companies has averaged 6.7 percent per year, and the stocks of those companies have sold at an average price of 15 times earnings. If the price-earnings multiple in effect in early 1999 (32 times forward earnings) were to move over the next 10 years toward the long-term average of 15, the effect would be to reduce total return from stocks by about 2 percent annually. Taking the three components together produces a forecast of about 7 percent for average annual returns on stocks through 2007, according to Bogle. Forward earnings refers to earnings projected over the next 12 months.

If you take an optimistic view that the economy has moved into a period of higher growth, with future corporate earnings rising by 9 percent annually and the price of stocks averaging 20 times earnings, annual returns might average 13 percent per year over the next 10 years. On the other hand, if problems persist in the Asian economies and if our economy enters a period of slower growth, then corporate earnings may experience a slower growth, perhaps at 4 percent a year. This might result in stocks being priced at 10 times earnings, well below the long-term average. If this pessimistic scenario came to pass, returns over the next 10 years could be minuscule, maybe at an annual average of just 1 percent.

The future will likely not match any of these scenarios, but it will continue to confound the pundits as it always has. For instance, after the stock market's huge advance in 1995, it was widely believed that the market would have to struggle to produce a positive return in 1996. Instead, it continued its astounding run in 1996, 1997, and again in 1998. The Dow Jones Industrial Average, which was at 3,838 at the beginning of 1995, advanced to 9,181 at the end of 1998, more than doubling for a gain of 139 percent!

IN A NUTSHELL

The stock market's current valuations are high by most traditional yardsticks of value. Thus, the risks of investing in common stocks have increased along with the sharp rise in prices over recent years. Consider these high valuations when forming your expectations for future returns.

CHAPTER *16*

Handling Stock Market Volatility

The recent volatility of the equity markets has been enough to challenge the resolve of even some disciplined long-term investors. But it is during times such as these that discipline counts the most. It may seem cold comfort to hear financial experts on television reminding people that the stock market has experienced similar volatility before, only to go on to reach new highs over the long term, but this is what the history of the stock market shows us. So while the past is not predictive of the future, a diversified portfolio of stocks is one of the best investment vehicles for long-term growth opportunities. It may be difficult to keep focused on long-term goals during periods of short-term volatility, but the ability to do this is one of the most common characteristics of successful investors.

The ups and downs of the stock market made headlines in recent years. Through July 17, 1998, U.S. stocks gained an astounding 23.3 percent as measured by the Standard & Poor's 500-stock index (S&P 500). But the gains from those six and a half months were wiped out over the next six weeks. Sharp price fluctuations—especially declines—can be unsettling for anyone but may be especially unnerving for the millions of people who began investing only during the 1990s, a period of unusually good returns for stocks. It's natural to be alarmed when the value of your investment account drops. But it's also important to understand that there's no way to pursue the rewards of investing without enduring the risks of price fluctuations that can be both severe and unpredictable.

The U.S. stock market endured three declines of approximately 10 percent or more in the 18 months ended August 1998. Such downturns may make it seem that the stock market has become unusually volatile. Not so. Recent volatility in the S&P 500 is high only in comparison with the unusually placid period of the mid-1990s. Recent declines have been steep, especially for small-company stocks, for example, which fell more than 30 percent from April through August 1998. Internationally, emerging markets have plummeted, with an average decline of nearly 40 percent during the first eight months of 1998.

The important lesson for investors is that big price swings simply come with the territory.

What Causes Market Volatility?

Although commentators are quick to offer reasons for the rise or fall of stocks, these are often just guesses. Markets are affected by the interplay of countless forces. Among the factors that influence stock prices, for example, are interest rates, inflation, corporate earnings, economic growth rates, and the strength or weakness of the dollar. Domestic and international politics also move markets. And just as powerful as all these, at least over short periods, is investor psychology, which is as mercurial as human behavior itself.

Finally, all of these elements—and the way they interact—are constantly shifting. So it's easy to see why pinpointing just what causes a market downturn or rally is often impossible. However, over the long run, it is *investment fundamentals* that determine the returns from stocks.

For stocks, long-term returns reflect basic fundamentals: A company's sales, earnings, and dividends will determine, over the long haul, how its stock price fares. The fact that the economy and corporate profits have grown over time explains the long-term rise in U.S. stock prices. But the decades-long uptrend has not been a straight line. Individual companies falter or fail, even as others prosper. And both the economy and corporate profits go through down cycles, some of which are severe.

Is the Market's Decline a Buying Opportunity?

There is no way to know for sure. At any given moment, some pundits can make a persuasive case for why the market's next move will be up, while others can make an equally plausible argument that it is headed down.

But your investment decisions should not be based on the opinions of the so-called experts. Nor should you make significant decisions based on recent market events, whether they seem favorable or unfavorable. The mix of holdings in your investment portfolio should be based on your time horizon, your objective for the portfolio, your financial situation, and your tolerance for risk.

Some investors believe in buying on dips—investing substantial sums after the market declines by, say, 10 or 20 percent. But declines can get steeper than 10 or 20 percent, and they can last a long time. For example, the 1973–1974 bear market lasted 22 months, during which the S&P 500 fell nearly 50 percent. Investors who bought on the dips were then likely to run out of money or faith long before the market began its slow climb back.

If your plan calls for you to make regular purchases, don't alter it until you have carefully reviewed all the key factors: the time horizon and your objectives, financial situation, and risk tolerance. If none of these factors has changed, why alter your investment program? In short, once you have developed a plan, stick to it.

Why Not Sell and Wait for Things to Settle Down?

After a market slide, the idea of selling your holdings and sitting on the sidelines until the markets are calmer is alluring. But it is rarely successful. No bell rings to tell you when to get in or out of the market.

Financial markets simply don't move in reliably predictable patterns. Yes, they move up and down. But market cycles aren't as regular as clockwork, and there's no surefire system to profit from timing these movements. Many investors—expert and amateur—have tried their hand at market timing. Few, if any, have succeeded regularly for long.

Remember, to profit from market timing, you must be right twice: once in choosing when to sell and once in choosing when to buy. And to succeed, you must be right often enough to overcome any tax and transaction costs related to your moves.

Finally, before reacting to market volatility, realize that in trying to avoid one risk, you may run into another. If you rush away from stocks and shift all your money into bonds, for example, you face interest rate risk—the possibility that rates will rise and bond prices will fall. Put your money into safe investments like money market funds or bank accounts, and inflation may erode your returns so that you fall far short of your long-term goals.

What Should You Do?

First, recognize that market volatility is an inescapable part of investing. Recognize, too, that for most people, investing is not optional—it is a necessity to pay for such worthy goals as your retirement or your children's education.

Once you accept these facts, you are ready to tailor your mix of stocks, bonds, and cash investments to weather the market's ups and downs. As you do, consider these four points:

Focus on Time, Not Timing

Your time horizon—the length of time until you expect to need the money from an investment—should be the first consideration. Focus on the time you are investing, not on timing the markets.

The shorter your time horizon, the greater emphasis you should place on price stability and on avoiding volatile assets. For example, money that you expect to need within a year or two should be held in relatively stable investments, such as money market funds, bank CDs, or short-term bond funds. For long-term goals, emphasize longer-term investments, such as stock funds and bond funds. The risk of steep short-term price declines in stocks and longer-term bonds makes them an unwise choice for short-term goals—you may need the money just after the market has plunged.

On the other hand, time is the ally of the long-term investor in stocks. Time can tame volatility. As your time horizon lengthens, you have less to fear from short-term price fluctuations in pursuit of the higher returns that stocks have historically provided. Stock returns for 1-year periods since 1960 have ranged from +37.4 percent to –26.5 percent, a spread of roughly 64 percentage points. However, over 20-year periods, the spread between the highest return (+16.6 percent annually) and the lowest (+6.8 percent annually) narrowed to less than 10 percentage points.

Construct a Balanced Portfolio

Although you can't escape volatility, you can moderate it by choosing a mix of assets—stocks, bonds, and cash reserves. A balanced mix means you won't earn the peak return from any one type of asset but neither will you have all your eggs in the basket that takes the biggest fall.

Returns on each type of asset can vary considerably from year to year, but they don't usually move up and down in lockstep. When stocks fall, bond prices may hold steady or rise. And cash investments add stability that is vital for emergency needs.

Another big advantage of having a balanced portfolio is that it can help you keep your cool. During a sharp decline in stocks, for example, it may be comforting to see that your bonds or cash investments are holding up relatively well (and providing a flow of cash distributions).

Have a Plan and Stick to It

Once you decide on a program that fits your needs and financial situation, stick to your plan. Be wary of changing it in response to the latest news or the opinion of an investment guru. Bear in mind that market commentary tends to focus on short-term trends and events and doesn't take into account the vastly different circumstances affecting each investor. After all, when it comes to knowing your time horizon, goals, and financial situation, *you* are the expert.

Staying on course with your plan can be difficult. During a rising market, the temptation is to add to your winners by investing new cash in them or by shifting money out of other assets. And during a down market, you may have a powerful urge to sell the losers and put your money elsewhere. However, by following the market's trends, you could be abandoning the investment program that best fits your needs in the long run.

Don't Run with the Herd

Although it's not easy when the markets are skyrocketing or plunging, try to maintain a long-term focus. You need to recognize—in advance—that markets are subject to both manic highs and depressive lows. Although fundamentals propel the markets over the long term, psychology can be in the driver's seat for shorter periods, even for years at a time.

And attitudes can change radically. During the 17-year bull market that began in August 1982, the dominant attitude of U.S. investors toward stocks went from intense pessimism to gleeful optimism. In the early 1980s, the bear markets of the 1970s were fresh in investors' minds, and many Americans viewed stocks as just too risky. At the same time, high interest rates were making short-term investments, such as money market funds and bank CDs, seem like sure, safe bets.

IN A NUTSHELL

It may be difficult to keep focused on long-term goals during periods of short-term volatility, but the ability to do this is one of the most common characteristics of successful investors. Understanding that the prevailing wisdom has often been wrong may help you to keep from being swept along by the emotion of the moment—whether euphoria or despair. Although financial markets are notoriously fickle, your approach to investing should be reasoned and steadfast. Have a plan. Stick to it.

Growth Stocks versus Value Stocks

A debate in academic and investing communities about whether it is better to invest in growth stocks or in value stocks is ongoing. Growth stocks are generally considered to be those with lower-than-average dividend yields and higher-than-average price-earnings and price-book ratios. Value stocks are those that offer higher-than-average dividend yields, lower-than-average price-earnings and price-book ratios, and are often perceived to be out of favor with investors.

Dividend yield is a popular value indicator. The dividend yield of a stock is calculated by simply dividing the annual dividend paid by the price. A stock trading at $100 per share and paying a dividend of $1.40 has a dividend yield of 1.4 percent (about the dividend yield on the S&P 500 in early 1999).

The price-earnings (PE) ratio, also known as the multiple, is calculated by dividing a stock's price by its earnings per share. Thus, a stock trading at $50 with earnings of $2 per share has a PE of 25. Many investors argue that the only earnings value to use in computing this number is the earnings for the last fiscal year. Others believe earnings for the current year are better. Still other investors believe the PE should be based on estimates for the next fiscal year.

Like the PE, price-to-book value (P/BV) is calculated by dividing a stock's price by its book value. The lower the result, the better. Some investors believe the P/BV is a better measure of value to use because they believe it yields better performance. As opposed to earnings representing a future flow of income to the investor, book value represents an estimate of liquidation value. Book value is not a very accurate estimate of liquidation value, but it provides a fairly comparable number within industries and companies of relatively common age.

To analyze how stocks come to be valued in the marketplace, let's first consider the question: What is wealth? According to John Rutledge, an economist and chairman of Rutledge & Company, "We measure wealth by asset values, defined as what people are willing to pay today to own claims on future income streams." This is true whether the future income is royalties, coupons on bonds, dividends on stocks, or rents on properties. But not all income streams are priced the same. Growing income streams are worth more than static ones, and reliable income streams are worth more than uncertain ones. In short, not all income streams are equally valuable.

Growth Stocks

Growth stocks have been ascendant in recent years. Over the three-year period ended September 30, 1998, the growth stock component of the S&P 500 earned 26.8 percent annually versus 18.1 percent for the value stocks in the index. Growth stocks, reflecting high expectations for future appreciation, typically sell at above-average prices in relation to earnings, dividends, and book value. What are the reasons?

- *Innovation pays.* In today's economy, brains matter much more than brawn. Many prominent growth stocks base their success on technological, scientific, or marketing advances, less tangible but potentially far more profitable than such capital-intensive assets as mines and factories. Innovations such as new medicines and computer software can be patented and powerful retail brands are copyrighted, allowing owners of these products and technologies to charge higher prices and keep profits growing.
- *Taxes matter.* Growth stocks tend to get a larger proportion of their total return from capital appreciation than do value stocks. This is because fast-growing companies typically pay low or no dividends, choosing instead to reinvest their profits in research, marketing, or expansion. Dividends are ordinary income to the investor and are taxed at a top rate of 39.6 percent, whereas long-term capital gains are subject to a top tax rate of 20 percent. So people investing in taxable accounts are likely to continue to

favor low-yielding growth stocks, which may be more tax friendly than higher-yielding value stocks.

- *Reliability is prized.* Many of the top growth stocks have proven track records of providing solid earnings growth year after year. Investors like this reliability, and it is why they have been willing to pay higher PE ratios to own these stocks. Low inflation and low interest rates make reliable growth stocks even more attractive, because they raise the current value that investors place on any given level of projected future earnings.

Value Stocks

Value stocks don't always lag, as they have recently. Even after growth stocks' recent hot streak, longer-term results for the groups are similar. For the 15 years ended September 30, 1998, value stocks earned an annual average of 15.7 percent versus 16.8 percent for growth stocks. Value stocks are often considered out of favor with investors and have below-average prices based on their earnings, dividends, and book value. Here are some reasons why they may return to favor:

- *Markets lean to the mean.* Stock market returns tend to revert to long-term norms. Periods of unusually high returns tend to be followed by periods of subpar returns, not only for the entire market, but for segments within it. So history suggests that value stocks will again have their day—though no one can say when.
- *Surprises can be pleasant.* Value stocks as a group generally trade at lower prices (in relation to earnings, dividends, and book value) because investors have relatively modest expectations for their future growth. Conversely, growth stocks typically carry high price tags because investors assume that past growth will continue indefinitely. Yet long-range forecasts of corporate earnings are notoriously poor. With expectations low, value stocks don't have to perform miracles to deliver pleasant earnings surprises and enjoy price appreciation.
- *Dividends still count.* Spectacular price increases during bull markets may make dividends seem irrelevant, but their role in long-term returns is anything but trivial. Even during such a phenomenal period as the ten years ended September 30, 1998, dividends accounted for about 30 percent of the S&P 500's cumulative

---

FIGURE 17.1 / A COMPARISON OF GROWTH AND VALUE STOCKS, 1963–1998

JULY 1963– JUNE 1998	LARGE GROWTH STOCKS	LARGE VALUE STOCKS	SMALL GROWTH STOCKS	SMALL VALUE STOCKS
Annual return	11.4%	15.3%	12.3%	17.9%
Annual volatility*	18.8	15.3	28.0	23.1

---

*The standard deviation of annual returns

return of 393 percent. If future returns decline toward long-term averages, dividends will matter even more. When stock prices are static or falling, dividends are the only positive source of returns. Although overall dividend yields are near historic lows, the 2 percent yield of the S&P 500's value stocks is nearly twice that of its growth stocks.

Should You Invest in Growth, Value, or Both?

Over the 35-year period from July 1963 to June 1998, value stocks (those with the lowest prices relative to book value) in the United States outperformed growth stocks and had lower volatility than growth stocks, as shown in Figure 17.1.

Those observers who come down on the side of market inefficiency point to the lower volatility of value stocks as proof that they are less risky than growth stocks. They also point to the lower downside risk of value stocks in many (but not all) of the down market years, as measured by the S&P 500. Figure 17.2 shows how value stocks did versus growth stocks in calendar years in which the market was down.

For investors with long investment time horizons, a value-only portfolio should generate higher returns with less volatility and downside risk. But these investors should understand that in any given year, or even several years in a row, it is probable that growth stocks will outperform, which is the main reason why many advisers recommend a combination of the asset classes.

FIGURE 17.2 / VALUE STOCKS VERSUS GROWTH STOCKS IN DOWN
MARKET YEARS

CALENDAR YEAR	S&P 500	LARGE GROWTH STOCKS	LARGE VALUE STOCKS	SMALL GROWTH STOCKS	SMALL VALUE STOCKS
1967	−10.1%	−11.0%	− 5.2%	− 6.4%	− 5.5%
1969	− 8.5	+ 0.6	−16.0	−23.9	−24.9
1973	−14.7	−20.3	− 2.8	−39.1	−26.0
1974	−26.5	−30.0	−22.4	−33.4	−18.1
1977	− 7.2	− 9.1	+ 0.8	+20.3	+21.8
1981	− 4.9	− 7.9	+11.2	− 4.1	+10.5
1990	− 3.2	+ 1.4	−13.9	−18.1	−20.8

How to Pick Stocks

Before you make your stock selections, it can be helpful to learn what investment analysts—at least those among them who have the best records of forecasting and picking winners—think will happen in the market. You can get a reasonable idea of that by reading the financial press and investment advisory newsletters.

You probably will benefit from reading sophisticated market guides, such as Standard & Poor's *Stock Guide* and *The Value Line Investment Survey,* and by using stock screening services online (see Chapter 4). These guides often are available free at your public library. They can help you find stocks with certain promising characteristics:

- Scout for stocks owned by fewer than five big institutional investors. These shares, while risky, often tend to rise faster than others. You can find out how many institutions hold an issue by looking it up in Standard & Poor's *Stock Guide.*
- Look for shares of well-established firms that pay high dividends relative to stocks in general, especially relative to stocks of companies in the same industry.
- Search also for stocks whose prices are low relative to their earnings. Newspaper stock tables show PE ratios based on the previous 12 months' earnings. For a better guide, use the ratio based on analysts' estimates of future earnings, published in *The Value Line Investment Survey.*

- Try to catch a fallen star, a stock that has fallen victim to bad news. You can spot these unfortunates in daily newspaper lists of stocks reaching 52-week lows. To find out whether the company is reeling from only a temporary setback instead of a terminal problem, look for long-term debt that is not greater than 40 percent of the company's total capitalization and less than 10 percent of annual sales. Aggressive new management, significant cost reductions, and the introduction of potentially profitable products are other signs of a potential comeback.

Remember, though, that low stock prices don't automatically mean value, as buyers of commercial bank stocks in 1990 learned to their sorrow. The median decline in 1990 of the share prices of the 50 largest banks was 36 percent, despite the fact that the prices were at depressed levels. Your margin of safety will come from buying healthy companies at attractive prices. *Healthy* means low debt with returns on equity of more than 15 percent. *Attractive* means that the stocks are selling at or below the market's average PE multiple and at a 25 to 50 percent discount to book value.

Sometimes you can find good buys on Wall Street by making a commonsense evaluation of the people, products, and services you encounter on Main Street. Many successful small investors discover that personal experience leads them to stock market winners. Your children might direct you to a new fast-food chain that is packed with hungry youngsters. Perhaps the chain's stock is worth a taste. Or you might detect a changing pattern in sales at your job. An investment opportunity may be behind it.

Investing in what you know firsthand lets you exploit two of your best assets: your experience and your own good judgment. But don't invest before first finding out more facts. Excellent products and services can come from poorly run, unprofitable companies. A personal encounter with a single product tells you nothing about a firm's other lines of business. They may not be as terrific. Use your experience, but don't let it do the whole job.

You should do the same kind of research you would do with any investment. Ask, for example: Does the company have a hoard of cash, real estate, oil reserves, or other assets that might catch the eye of a takeover artist or make the market take a second look? The most convenient sources for answers are usually *The Value Line Investment Survey* (www.valueline.com) or Morningstar (www.morningstar.net).

IN A NUTSHELL

If you have a long investment time horizon, a value-only portfolio should generate higher returns with less volatility and downside risk. But you should understand that in any given year, or
even several years in a row, it is probable that growth stocks will
outperform value stocks—the main reason why many advisers
recommend a combination of the two asset classes.

Should You Buy Stocks on Margin?

Sooner or later many investors come across the concept of buying on margin, or using borrowed money to purchase stock to get extra oomph in their portfolio. But new investors should think twice before taking the plunge.

Brokers are only too happy to lend you money to buy stocks and bonds if you open a margin account. You have to put up only part of the securities' price, and your broker lends you the rest. You just sign a couple of forms, and your broker runs a routine credit check on you. Brokers are eager to approve your application because margin accounts lead to more business and higher profits for them.

You can come out ahead in rising markets because you put up only 50 percent of the cost of your stocks and 25 percent of the cost of your bonds. So your money works at least twice as hard for you. The interest that you pay on your margin loan is not only relatively low but is also deductible from your taxable income up to the amount of your net investment income for the year.

Consider this scenario: It's late October 1998. After a sharp downturn over the past several months, the market has turned up. You find a stock you like. It's speculative, but you're willing to take the risk. The name is eBay. It's part of the red-hot Internet group in which Amazon.com and Yahoo! are doing so well. You have $10,000 to invest in your margin account. The quote on eBay is 50. With margin you can borrow money from your broker to buy additional eBay shares. Using

100 percent of your margin capability, you have buying power of $20,000—$10,000 of your money and $10,000 from the broker.

You buy $20,000 of eBay and get 400 shares. The price of eBay's stock soars to 73⅜ the next day, and it's off to the races. The price sky-rockets to 234 by November 24. You cash out, selling 400 shares and getting back $93,600. By using margin, your profit is $73,600 ($93,600 minus $10,000 of your capital and $10,000 to pay back the loan). If you hadn't used margin, your profit would only be $36,800.

Sound easy? Maybe too easy. You look brilliant. But wait a minute. New investors must be careful when borrowing money from a brokerage and using it to buy additional stock. It's a two-edged sword. If the price of the stock were to go down, the invested money would decline twice as fast. In the stock market crash of 1987, many stocks fell 40 percent or more in just a few days. Any account margined to the hilt suffered horrendous losses.

Margin isn't free: You pay interest on the borrowed money. The rate is marked up from the broker loan rate. A typical interest rate charged in early 1999 was 9.75 percent on a loan of less than $50,000. For larger loans the rate may be as much as two percentage points less.

It's wise not to venture out on margin until you've made several profitable trades. The best time to use margin is during the early phase of a new bull market. Once you recognize a new bear market, though, you should get off margin immediately and raise cash. An account should not be fully margined all the time. When progress is being made during a bull market, heavy margin can be used. But when a correction sets in you should reduce your margin by selling shares.

It's important to remember that it is a market of stocks, not a stock market. You must watch your stock positions and respond accordingly. Don't take solace in the general market averages. During the market retreat that occurred in 1998, many stocks turned lower well before the Dow industrials revealed serious weakness in July and August.

If your stock rises—great! If it rises enough, you could sell some shares, pay off the margin loan and come out ahead. But if the gains in your stock don't cover your interest payments, you lose money. And if the stock price falls, you could suffer in two ways. Not only would your investment dwindle, but you could receive a call from your broker—a so-called margin call—to put up more cash.

A margin call occurs when the value of your collateral falls below a certain percent of your total purchase price—usually 30 to 35 percent. If the worth of your holdings drops under that level, your broker will demand that you deliver enough cash or other securities to bring your collateral back up to the required amount. If you can't deliver—sometimes by the next day—the broker will sell your stock, take back what was lent you, and collect interest.

Before you decide to borrow on margin, ask yourself this key question: "Do I believe in the shares so wholeheartedly that I would be willing to borrow money even from a bank in order to own them?" If not, a margin account is not for you. If you do invest on margin, keep a close eye on your stocks. Check the prices often. You don't want a margin call to take you by surprise.

Protecting Yourself While on Margin

To protect yourself if you think the market is heading for a fall, you can buy what's called a *put option,* which is the right to sell a stock at a specified price within a set period of time, usually up to eight months, to the seller of the put. If the price of your stock drops enough, the put option will become more valuable. Then you can sell the option to offset the losses on your stock. Example: In January 1999 the share price of ABC Steel is up to $80, and you believe that's too high. So you buy a put on 100 shares of ABC at $80, coming due on September 1, 1999. Lo and behold, the stock does drop to $60 on September 1. You cash in your put and collect $80 per share, or a total of $8,000 for the 100 shares. But those shares are worth only $6,000 in the market, so you've gained $2,000 minus whatever you paid for the put.

For extra insurance, you can instruct your broker to sell your shares automatically if they fall to a certain price; this is called a *stop order.* Choose the price at which you would no longer want to own the stock and advise your broker to sell at that level. Then if your shares fall without your noticing, your broker will sell them and prevent your losing more money.

It's extremely important to have strict rules when using margin. Here are a few guidelines:

- Use margin only during bull markets.
- Never use margin to buy in declining markets.
- Have clear sell rules for each stock.
- Borrow less than the maximum.
- Check your stock prices daily.
- Never use margin to buy more shares of a stock that is falling.

There are also some personal considerations for you to keep in mind:

- Don't use margin if you can't accept the risk. The value of your portfolio rises—and falls—twice as fast on full margin.
- Don't use margin if you don't like debt.
- Don't use margin with small accounts. You are more likely to concentrate your holdings in fewer stocks and that makes using margin riskier.
- Don't use margin for long-term investing. Slower-moving big cap stocks, which are favorites of the buy-and-hold investor, won't move fast enough to justify the interest charges on a margin loan. A big cap stock might move up 15 or 20 percent in a year, but interest charges would almost cut the return in half.

Not all securities are marginable. Stocks selling under $5 usually can't be margined. The New York Stock Exchange can set special loan limits for individual issues that show unusual volume or price fluctuations, which discourages speculation.

Finally: Never answer a margin call. If you have an account on margin and a stock declines to where you must put up more money to maintain the position, don't do it. Sell the stock. It may be painful, but the market is telling you that you are on the wrong path.

IN A NUTSHELL

Never let your dream turn into a nightmare by using margin. Always have a disciplined plan before even considering buying on margin. It's a good idea to have it down in writing and refer to it often.

Day Trading Online

The Internet has changed everything. On a Friday late in 1998, shares of Onsale, a Web-based auction service, rocketed more than 60 percent. Books-a-Million and Connect, both Web-based businesses, posted even more spectacular gains. Most professional investors and market experts are not overly concerned about this kind of activity. The volume of shares that such companies make available for trading is relatively small and thus has little effect on the overall health of the market. In addition, they say, Internet stocks are widely, and correctly, regarded as high-risk investments.

But what was noteworthy about the trading action on that day was that it was caused by day traders—primarily individual investors trading online—who rely on quick market fluctuations to turn a profit. And these individuals dominated the trading volume in at least a few high-technology growth stocks on that day.

For the first time, anyone with a computer, a connection to the global network, and the requisite ironclad stomach for risk has the information, tools, and access to transaction systems required to play the stock market, a game that was once the purview of an elite few. Those who believe that this kind of decentralization of power is the primary benefit of an Internet-based economy believe this is good news. But one has to wonder about the unintended consequences of such a fundamental shift.

Some studies show that the number of individuals jumping onto the Internet increases by thousands every day; as technology improves, that number is likely to rise even faster. Information—especially the kind of information that fuels stock trading, like real-time quotes and company data—is on the verge of becoming ubiquitous. Couple that with the likelihood that as more individuals make money in a booming stock market, word of mouth, spread in chat rooms and newsgroups via the Internet itself, is likely to attract still more day traders. The growth will be exponential. Some online brokers are already projecting that they will have to double or triple their technology investments to keep up with increased volume from Internet traders.

Some investors are anticipating the near-term effects of day trading on the Internet economy itself, which is fueled in large part by the hefty prices commanded by Internet-related stocks. These price effects have consequences. A prolonged run-up in stock prices could prove to be a double whammy for Internet companies. For one thing, it will become increasingly difficult to hire talented managers if they believe that the shares are so overpriced that the stock options being offered them are likely to be considerably devalued when the market comes to its senses. If companies reset the options at a lower, more attractive price, institutional investors, who hold most of the market's stock and tend to invest in assets rather than concepts, will balk. Today, institutional investors, as well as program traders who move large blocks of stock in a single computer-guided transaction, affect the overall stability of the larger market. But if individual trading on the Internet continues to grow at its current pace, it is possible to imagine a situation in which the market as we know it today cannot absorb the shock. In the short term, the problem may solve itself. Not too many people have the stomach for day trading and the situation will eventually settle.

Day Trading Today

Day trading is not for the faint of heart. Like other forms of investing, it doesn't come with a guarantee that future returns will mimic any favorable ones of the past. And because day trading is highly speculative and can easily swallow up large chunks of cash, experts say it is not an appropriate investment strategy for, say, saving for retirement or college.

Getting started can be very expensive as well. For example, although some day trading firms let a customer get started with just

$25,000 in an account, Broadway Trading (www.broadwaytrading. com) requires at least $75,000. Several day trading firms say that even well-padded investors can expect to wait six months before they begin making money. And while they are waiting, it is common to lose tens of thousands of dollars. For that reason, some firms recommend that new day traders trade only in lots of 200 shares at a time.

Other costs can add up quickly as well. Investors who trade full-time from home, for example, can expect to pay an extra $400 to $700 a month in phone costs alone as part of dialing into a company's trading system. To cut connection costs, some day trading firms offer their proprietary services through the Internet. To ensure reliability, the firms will also recommend an Internet service provider.

Unlike traditional online investing where investors hang on to stocks for months or even years, day trading is a fast and furious game of speculation that can mean jaw-dropping returns but is also notoriously risky. One strategy hinges on the ability to move quickly in exploiting spreads, the tiny differences that typically exist between a stock's bid price (how much stock dealers are willing to pay for a share) and its offered price (the price at which dealers are willing to sell a share). Spreads are expressed in fractions of one thirty-seconds of a dollar, a little more than 3¢.

Large volume traders, like Wall Street investment houses, have been able to take advantage of spreads for years, pocketing the difference between what they charge small investors for a stock and what they actually pay for it. But only recently have independent investors themselves had access to the computer technology that lets them track the prices bid and offered for a stock and post their own bids. As a result, even small investors can trade within a stock's spread either by using computers in a day trading firm or in their home.

Here's how it works: Let's say an investor is sitting at a computer screen at a day trading office and notices that the price bid for a stock is $64.375, and it is being offered for $64.75. Attracted by the spread, the investor puts in a bid and is able to buy 4,000 shares of the stock at $64.4375 (total purchase price: $257,750) and then, within seconds, turns around and sells those shares at $64.6875 (total selling price $258,750). The profit: $1,000.

If day trading sounds easy, it isn't. Traders can easily lose thousands of dollars in a few minutes—or they can make as much. Day traders may suffer in an extended bear market, but they can benefit from volatility, which often accompanies a market's downturn. Stock volatility, however, is not the only key to successful day trading. Speed is important; some traders carry out 1,000 trades a day. And because the spreads are so small, stock volume is important as well; most day traders trade thousands of shares of any particular stock at a time. To make $14,000 in one day, for example, one day trader traded some 390,000 shares of stock.

A few years ago, independent investors might not have been able to do that kind of trading. At that time, only traders for large institutional investors had access to the information needed to do day trading as well as the fast, low-cost execution technology. If smaller investors wanted to play, they usually had to go through an intermediary like a broker; the process typically ate up precious minutes, and brokers charged high commissions.

The Nasdaq exchange, which generally has more volatile stocks and larger spreads, has made itself available to small investors through the SOES—the Small Order Execution System. The SOES is an automatic system so all orders are processed, but it has some disadvantages for spread players, like a ceiling of 1,000 shares per trade and time restrictions on multiple stock purchases. Such restrictions are not found in another technology day traders use: electronic communication networks (ECNs), which give smaller investors a chance to post their own stock bids. ECNs don't have time restrictions and limits on the size of transactions. The result is that day trading has soared in popularity, spawning Web sites, dozens of day trading classes, and specialized trading firms that offer the SOES and ECNs in large trading rooms and remotely, with direct access through modems or through Internet sites.

Experts estimate that there are some 100 companies around the country that offer some form of day trading. Day trading firms make their money several ways. First, they charge commissions, usually between $10 and $25 per trade. Some firms charge, say, 2¢ per share of stock traded or $20 per thousand shares. Firms also charge for remote access to their systems; for example, $250 a month.

Many firms charge for extensive training sessions, some of them mandatory before trading and some just strongly recommended. Such training sessions typically cost about $1,500. Optional full-time courses are available for $5,000 as well as occasional day trading "boot camp" sessions for $3,000.

Industry sources say that about two-thirds of day trading customers come from outside the financial industry. And most of them trade from computers at home. Home computer users can do day trading more easily than ever before. To gain direct access to some day trading systems, investors need to have only a phone line, an IBM-compatible Pentium computer, a color monitor, and a modem.

Day trading sites available on the Internet are a growing avenue as well. But many day traders say that for carrying out hundreds of trades quickly and reliably each day, they prefer logging directly onto the more sophisticated online trading systems that are available from firms like Broadway Trading (www.broadwaytrading.com), Momentum Securities Management Company (www.soes.com), All-Tech Investment Group (www.attain.com), OTC Day Trading (www.otcday trading.com), Astrikos Trading (www.astrikos.com), and Castle Online (www.castleonline.com). Additional day trading firms can be found at Investorama (www.investorama.com/daytrading).

Experiences of Some Day Traders

According to Wall Street Access (www.wsaccess.com), an online broker that caters to day traders, Bill Huggin is a self-taught day trader. He learned the old-fashioned way: by trial and error. In the five years he's been trading, he has learned how to survive and even thrive on the ups and downs of the market. Now he supports his family with his trading profits and runs a Web site where other traders—from novice to expert—can learn from his experience in the market. Huggin places about ten trades a day.

The strategy he follows involves searching out volatile stocks and getting in—and out—fast. He says he rarely stays in a position for more than ten minutes! In making his moves, he looks at technical data to find opportunities like reflex rallies or breakouts. Mostly, Huggin trades technology stocks; almost everything he trades is on the Nasdaq. "I watch for opportunities where I can bottom fish—find a stock that has plummeted to a low and buy it real quick. If it doesn't turn around right away, within minutes, I sell anywhere from half to all of my position to cut my losses. Similarly, if the stock goes up, I will sell half and let some ride."

Huggin thinks it's critical for day traders to learn how to take a small loss. "It's better to get out with a manageable loss and live to trade another day." One strategy he recommends is going short against the box. Basically, you are long and short the same stock at the same time. (Note: You are long by actually owning a position in the stock; you are short by selling shares of the stock that you borrow from your broker.) When you want to exit the short-against-the-box position, you buy long shares of the stock. Be sure to tell your broker you want to be short against the box. Now you are hedged (your risk has been reduced). What this lets you do is sell a long position at any time without having to wait for an up bid. This is a powerful day trading strategy because it allows you to play a potential down move in a stock—that is, the stock you are short against the box—on an intraday basis at anytime. That can be critical to success as a day trader.

Not everyone makes money. Another day trader, from Glastonbury, Connecticut, has had a tough time hanging on. When he began trading stocks online from his home in 1996, his wife had recently died and he had quit a job in the computer industry to spend more time with his eight-year-old daughter. After taking a course from Broadway Trading, he moved into day trading. Two or three months later, however, he thought that he was losing too much money, perhaps because he was trading from home without the presence of trading colleagues who could offer valuable advice. So in September 1997, he began trading at a day trading office in Hartford. Even that move didn't produce the results he was banking on. Discouraged, he took a job with a financial services company. "In terms of making a profit," he said, "I would have been better off putting the money in a mutual fund."

Even successful day traders seem to be able to stand the pressure-cooker atmosphere only so long. One longtime day trader said his goal was to make a million dollars and retire at 30, when he might become a teacher. Another successful day trader is also reconsidering his priorities. His father taught him how to chart stocks when he was 11; and he now spends most of his time teaching other day traders instead of trading himself. He said: "Before I lost my father, he had four heart attacks and triple bypass surgery. I still have a need to day trade but not at the level I used to."

IN A NUTSHELL

Day trading is not for the fainthearted. It is highly speculative and can easily swallow up large chunks of your money. And getting started can be very expensive. Most day trading firms require at least $25,000 in your account. Experts say you can expect to wait several months before you begin making money, meanwhile possibly losing tens of thousands of dollars.

Bear Markets Can Bite You

Over the ten-year period through 1998, the stock market, as measured by the Standard & Poor's 500-stock index (S&P 500), provided investors with an average return of 19.2 percent, far outpacing the long-term historical average of 11 percent. In general, stock returns have been bountiful and the market has not suffered a severe or prolonged period of falling prices in quite some time. Protracted downturns, known in Wall Street as bear markets, can test the resolve of even the most seasoned investor. The stock market, for example, declined a stunning 48 percent over a nearly two-year period in the early 1970s.

Because no one can predict the timing or magnitude of future market movements with any degree of precision, the advent of the next bear market remains a mystery. Nonetheless, it is only prudent that you—especially if you have yet to experience a bear market—be in position to weather declines in the market over lengthy periods. This chapter provides some perspective on past bear markets and offers several guidelines on preparing your investment program for the next (and inevitable) extended market downturn.

A Bear Market Defined

Analysts aren't in complete agreement, but one generally accepted definition of a bear market in stocks is a price decline of 20 percent or more over at least a two-month period. By comparison, a market correction is usually defined as a sudden, sharp decline in stock prices that may last only a few days or weeks. A prime example of a market correction occurred in the summer of 1998 when the S&P 500, a widely accepted benchmark of the broad stock market, lost about 17 percent of its value in a six-week period.

Since 1956, nine downturns are generally regarded to have been bear markets with declines of nearly 20 percent or more, as measured by the S&P 500. Bear markets have occurred, on average, about once every four to five years. The average duration was 12 months—ranging from as short as 3 months to nearly 2 years, as shown in Figure 20.1.

What Causes Bear Markets?

It's difficult, if not impossible, to predict just what will precipitate a market plunge. It's an equally daunting task to foresee how investors will react to an initial decline in stock prices and what impact such reactions will have on the financial markets. Some professional and individual investors may view a temporary price drop as an opportunity to buy stocks at a discount, while others may see the same decline as the start of a deeper downturn.

Using history as a guide, one can discern some of the underlying causes of past bear markets. Iraq's invasion of Kuwait in 1990 touched off the most recent bear market in the U.S. stock market. The Persian Gulf crisis led to an escalation of oil prices, renewed fears of inflation, and a rise in interest rates—all of which, among other factors, sent stock prices reeling. Such a confluence of factors also accompanied the 1973–1974 stock market collapse. The country remained mired in economic stagflation, which stemmed primarily from the energy price increases resulting from the Arab oil embargo. The downturn was exacerbated by political upheavals associated with the Watergate saga and the winding down of the country's involvement in Vietnam.

The stock market, however, does not always mirror the state of the economy. The downturn in 1987 occurred during a period of economic advance, although the sharp rise in interest rates certainly contributed to the crash in stock prices. Conversely, the current leg of the

---

FIGURE 20.1 / BEAR MARKETS IN STOCKS FROM 1956 TO 1998

DATES	DURATION IN MONTHS	RECOVERY PERIOD IN MONTHS*	PERCENTAGE DECLINE
August 1956– October 1957	14.7	11.1	−21.6%
December 1961– June 1962	6.4	14.3	−28.0
February 1966– October 1966	7.9	6.9	−22.2
November 1968– May 1970	17.9	21.3	−36.1
January 1973– October 1974	20.7	69.4	−48.2
September 1976– March 1978	17.5	17.3	−19.4
January 1981– August 1982	19.2	2.3	−25.8
August 1987– December 1987	3.3	19.7	−33.5
July 1990– October 1990	2.9	4.3	−19.9

---

*Number of months until the market reached its previous high

prolonged bull market in stocks started in the early 1990s in the midst of a recession. Go figure.

Nonetheless, the relative strength of the stock market is tied to the general health of the economy as well as to political forces. Obviously, when the economic outlook or political landscape appears bright, investors tend to be optimistic about the prospects of corporate profits and are more willing to invest their money in stocks. When conditions sour, investors often forgo investing additional assets in stocks or sell their shares outright. Beyond fundamental economic factors, then, the sentiment of investors also exerts tremendous influence on the direction of the securities markets—both up and down. Figure 20.2 shows some of the positive and negative factors that influence investment in stocks.

Whatever the underlying causes, bear markets should be viewed as a regular part of investing. Moreover, the uncertainty surrounding the start, depth, and duration of market drops gives investors all the more reason to prepare—in advance—to ride out any declines.

FIGURE 20.2 / FACTORS THAT INFLUENCE STOCK PRICES

POSITIVE FACTORS	NEGATIVE FACTORS
An easy money policy imposed by the Federal Reserve	A tight money policy imposed by the Federal Reserve
A low or declining rate of inflation	A high or increasing rate of inflation
Low or declining interest rates	High or rising interest rates
Rising corporate profits	Declining or stagnant corporate profits
Political stability	Political instability or international conflict
High employment	High unemployment

A Perspective on Past Bear Markets

The worst bear market in stock market history occurred from September 1929 through July 1932, when stock prices fell some 86 percent. Rampant speculation, highly leveraged buying, and sheer panic ushered in a cataclysmic period in the financial markets that accompanied the Great Depression. Although regulatory changes make the recurrence of such a dramatic decline in stock prices unlikely, you would be well served by remembering that anything is possible in the securities markets.

In the post–World War II era, the worst bear market began in January 1973 and lasted roughly 21 months to October 1974, during which the market fell some 48 percent (as measured by the S&P 500). In dollar terms, an investor who had $10,000 invested in stocks experienced a loss of $4,800—nearly one-half of the portfolio's value. Furthermore, because inflation jumped significantly at the same time, the loss in terms of purchasing power was far greater.

Holding a balanced portfolio of stocks, bonds, and cash investments can cushion the decline of any one market. A portfolio composed of stocks and bonds fared much better during the 1973–1974 bear market; an investor holding 60 percent in stocks and 40 percent in bonds lost only $2,900. This elementary example demonstrates the benefits of diversifying your investment program across asset classes.

The heartening news to long-term investors is that the market eventually recovers from its declines. However, in most cases it can take some time. For example, following the 1973–1974 bear market (as shown in Figure 20.1), it took nearly eight years for the market to reach its precollapse peak.

Unfortunately, one of the more common mistakes made by investors during bear markets is to lose patience and sell at or near the bottom of the downturn. Many investors did just that in the 1973–1974 decline. Those who got out of stocks missed an extraordinary rebound in market performance. After declining to its low in October 1974, the market (as measured by the S&P 500) provided generous returns in the ensuing periods. Annual returns averaged 14.8 percent over the 10 years from 1975 through 1984, 16.6 percent over the 15 years from 1975 through 1989, and 14.6 percent over the 20 years from 1975 through 1994.

Along with maintaining patience in the midst of bear markets, you would be wise to guard against being fooled by false rallies. A bear market is not typically characterized by a straight-line decline in stock prices. Rather, the market's downward trend is likely to show intermittent bursts of stock price increases, which some investors mistakenly take as the return of a bull market. The 1973–1974 bear market was replete with these so-called sucker's rallies.

Finally, it is important to note that the bulk of major market movements—both up and down—often occur over brief periods. Over the past 70 years, the S&P 500 has dropped more than 7 percent in a single day on 14 different occasions, with the biggest one-day fall coming on October 19, 1987, when the S&P 500 closed down 20 percent. When stocks recover, it is common for the gains to be concentrated in a few days or weeks of extraordinary activity. Consequently, trying to time the markets by temporarily abandoning stocks requires a perfectly executed exit as well as an equally deft return—a nearly impossible feat.

Bear Market Rules of Survival

Bear markets are unquestionably trying times for investors. Here are some survival rules to help you manage your investments during the next market downturn:

- *Maintain your balance.* Hold a mix of stocks, bonds, and cash investments tailored to your objectives, time horizon, tolerance for risk, and overall financial situation. Cash investments such as CDs provide stability as well as liquidity for financial emergencies, whereas bonds offer steady income and can help dampen the swings in stock prices. Stocks have historically provided the highest long-term returns and the best long-term protection against inflation at the cost of greater price volatility. Periodically review your investment portfolio and make adjustments as necessary to keep your mix of investments in line with your goals.

- *Stay on an even keel.* It's human nature to become nervous and want to revise your investment mix at the first sign of trouble. Market downswings can cause even the most enthusiastic investors to have second thoughts. It pays, however, to remain focused on the long term. The markets run in irregular cycles in which good and bad markets come and go. Remember, you are trying to achieve a long-term goal, not to avoid a short-term loss.

- *Continue investing regularly.* If you invest regularly through an automatic investment plan or a 401(k) plan, continue making contributions. This strategy of dollar cost averaging enables you to put the market's natural volatility to work for you by lowering the average price you pay for your shares. (See Chapter 10 for a full discussion of this important subject.) It also reduces the risk of committing substantial assets at a time when the market is considered high.

- *Make gradual shifts (if necessary).* Resist the temptation to fundamentally alter your investment strategy simply because one component of your program heads downward. Most experts will tell you that moving your money from stocks and bonds to more conservative investments in hopes of avoiding a loss or finding a gain is seldom successful. And remember, too, that even though investment vehicles such as bank deposit accounts and CDs safeguard you against day-to-day fluctuations, they do little to preserve the spending power of your assets over time.

- *Consider the tax consequences of selling.* Many investors swore off stocks after the 1973–1974 debacle—selling out their entire equity holdings. Not only did these investors miss out on the market's eventual rally, but they most likely incurred a tax liability in doing so. Although it should not be your sole consideration, evaluate the tax consequences of your investment decisions. Given the tremendous advance in stock prices over the past 15 years, you may realize a significant capital gain when you sell shares at a higher price than you purchased them.

- *Set realistic expectations.* Stocks have provided handsome average returns of 20.2 percent per year (for the S&P 500) over the past ten years. The years 1995 through 1998 were particularly extraordinary with stocks returning 37.5 percent, 22.9 percent, 33.9 percent, and 28.6 percent, respectively, for each of those years. It's easy for investors to assume that the best projection of future returns is a replay of the recent past. It's more realistic, however, to expect less generous returns in the years ahead.

IN A NUTSHELL

This chapter is meant to raise a cautionary flag to stock market investors—to not predict the advent or severity of the next bear market. Nonetheless, stock prices are currently high by many traditional yardsticks of value, and the risk of investing in stocks is properly considered high at this point. The prudent investor understands this and is prepared to weather the market corrections and bear markets that are sure to come.

Online Direct Purchase Plans and DRIPs

Buying stock directly from a company used to be a privilege reserved for existing shareholders. But in recent years the barriers have been falling. By early 1999, companies offering so-called no-load stock purchase programs to first-time investors had risen to more than 500. And of those, nearly 100 permit online access to direct purchase of their stock. And the pace is picking up. In addition to companies that permit investors to buy their stock on a direct basis, well over 1,100 firms maintain dividend reinvestment plans.

Buying Stocks Direct

Direct investment plans let you buy stock direct from your favorite companies. With direct investment you have the power to

- buy stock without paying brokerage commissions;
- invest whole dollar amounts; and
- set up automatic monthly payments.

Many of the nation's leading corporations, such as BellSouth, Exxon, IBM, Intel, Johnson Controls, Merck, and Texaco, among others, sell their shares directly to investors through stock purchase and dividend reinvestment plans (DRIPs). For instance, Merck & Company, a leading research-driven pharmaceutical products and services company, offers its common stock for sale directly through the Merck Stock Investment Plan (www.merck.com), which is administered by Norwest Shareowner Services. The plan is available to investors who don't own Merck stock as well as to current shareholders and permits you to make an initial investment of as little as $350. Additional voluntary investments in minimum amounts of $50 can be made as often as weekly, or you can arrange for automatic monthly cash investments. All of or a percentage of your dividends may be automatically reinvested in additional shares of Merck common stock.

A similar plan, providing for online enrollment, is offered by IBM (www.ibm.com), the world's top provider of computer hardware, software, and services. The IBM plan is also available to investors who don't own IBM stock and is administered by EquiServe—First Chicago Trust Division. The plan requires a minimum initial investment of $500, and additional monthly investments can be made for as little as $50.

To invest in direct purchase plans (plans in which you can make your initial purchase directly), you must first obtain an enrollment form. The fastest way to get an enrollment form is through Netstock Direct (www.netstockdirect.com) and its Online Access program. You can fill out the form online and then print it out. Some companies are beginning to support electronic enrollment. If you can't find, or are unable to order, the plan materials online, just call the company's toll-free number for an enrollment form. Once you have obtained the form, fill it out and return it to the company along with your check for your initial investment. You won't receive stock certificates unless you request them; otherwise, your shares are held in book-entry form, just like a mutual fund.

A number of direct purchase plans have implemented fees in recent years that usually include a one-time enrollment fee (from $5 to $15) and per-purchase fees (usually $1 to $10 per purchase). Although fees may be creeping into these plans, however, plenty of quality companies still have very few or no fees on the buy side.

Dividend reinvestment plans, or DRIPs, allow long-term stock market investors who are in the accumulation phase of their investment plans to solve the problem of how to handle income. Dividends received by most individual shareholders are insufficient to buy additional shares economically. And yet, to maximize long-term return, buy-and-hold investors must continuously reinvest investment income. Today, more than 1,100 companies offer dividend reinvestment plans. A listing of these companies is published annually and may be obtained from the American Association of Individual Investors (www.aaii.org).

DRIPs are ideal for buy-and-hold investors and are a bonus for shareholders of companies with favorable long-term growth prospects. The plans are simple: Instead of sending cash dividends to participating investors, the company applies the cash dividends to the purchase of additional shares of company stock.

Participants enjoy several advantages:

- Dividend payments are put to work.
- Transaction costs are eliminated or held to a minimum.
- The additional shares are purchased gradually over time, an effective method of dollar cost averaging.

Special Features

Some company plans have the following special features that make them even more attractive:

- You may make optional cash payments to purchase additional shares through the plan.
- Participants are permitted to receive cash dividends on some of their shares while reinvesting dividends on the remaining shares.
- Shares purchased under the plan are available at discounts ranging from as little as 1 percent to as much as 10 percent.
- Brokerage costs and service fees for share purchases are paid for by the company rather than the participant.
- At some companies, investors with shares held by the transfer agent can borrow up to 50 percent of the value of their account at rates close to prime.
- Other services are making direct purchase/DRIP accounts sound more like brokerage accounts. Many companies now let investors redeem their shares by phone.

Most DRIPs require that you own shares registered in your name, that is, that you are a shareholder of record. That means your name must appear on the corporate records as the owner of the shares rather than allowing the shares to be held in the so-called street name by the broker or bank that may have bought the shares for you and who may be holding them for you. If your shares are held in street name, just ask your broker to transfer the shares to your name.

Usually the company will send you a DRIP plan description and an authorization card once you become a registered shareholder. You also can call the company's shareholder relations department or the DRIP agent to request these items. The prospectus or plan description provides information relating to eligibility requirements, plan options, costs, how and when purchases are made, how and when certificates are issued, and how you may withdraw from the plan.

How the Plans Work

Direct purchase plans and DRIPs are part of a corporation's overall shareholder relations effort and serve both existing and new shareholders. Some companies, such as utilities, have large investor relations departments and administer their own plans. Most companies, however, hire an outside agent to be the plan administrator.

The plan administrator maintains records, sends account statements to participants, provides certificates for shares on request, and liquidates participants' shares when they leave the plan. The agent also has the responsibility of buying company shares for the plan. When you join a plan, you sign a card that authorizes the agent to act on your behalf to purchase shares.

When shares are purchased, they are held by the plan and registered in the nominee name of the agent or plan trustee on behalf of the participants. An account is maintained for each participant under the plan. Most DRIP participants hold the company's shares in two places: Your original shares will be held by you or in the custody of a brokerage firm or bank, and the shares purchased through the plan will be held by the plan.

Some plans permit participants to deposit certificates of shares registered in their own name into their plan account for safekeeping at no cost or for a small fee. These shares are then treated in the same way as the other shares in a participant's account, thus making it possible to consolidate all your shares in one safe location.

Certificates for shares purchased under a plan normally are issued only on written request and often at no charge. Certificates also are issued when a participating shareholder wants to terminate participation.

Available Options

Full reinvestment of all shares of stock registered in a participant's name is standard under the basic direct purchase plan or DRIP. But under some plans, it's not necessary to reinvest all dividends; instead, participants may reinvest dividends on a portion of their registered shares, while receiving cash dividends on the remaining shares, often referred to as a partial reinvestment option.

Many plans permit participants to buy additional shares by making cash payments directly to the plan, sometimes in large allowable amounts. Often referred to as an optional cash payment, this option offers participants a low-cost way to build a sizable holding in a company. The payments are optional, and participants are not committed to making periodic cash payments. However, there are minimums and usually a maximum for each payment made. Because interest is not paid on payments received in advance, you should find out approximately when the plan invests cash payments it receives.

Some companies also offer a cash payment–only option, which allows registered shareholders to make cash investments without requiring them to reinvest dividends on the shares they are holding, although they may if they wish.

Costs of Direct Purchase Plans and DRIPs

Service charges and prorated brokerage commissions are the two forms of costs that plan participants may encounter. Service charges cover administrative costs and generally are made on each transaction. Costs can be held down by a participant combining cash payment with a dividend reinvestment transaction, for charges usually are capped at a maximum of $3 to $5. Brokerage costs paid by the plan when you buy shares on the open market are at institutional rates, considerably lower than the rate you'd typically pay as an individual investor.

Many companies cover all the costs for share purchases from both optional cash payments and reinvested dividends. Some companies assess service charges, others prorate brokerage costs, while still others charge participants for both. The plan prospectus or description spells out which of the many variations apply in each case.

When you terminate participation, some plans will sell shares for you if you wish instead of sending you certificates. Your cost is usually any prorated brokerage commission, a lower-cost choice than selling through a broker. Some plans will sell some of your plan shares for you even when you are not terminating. Again, check the prospectus or plan description.

Purchasing Shares

The plan prospectus or description spells out the source of share purchases under a DRIP or direct purchase plan.

The most common sources are the secondary market, a securities exchange where the shares are traded; in the over-the-counter market (OTC); or through negotiated transactions. In some cases, the source may be the company itself, using authorized but unissued shares of common stock or shares held in the company's treasury. An advantage to a participant when shares are purchased directly from the company is that there are no brokerage expenses to prorate.

For the company, plans that purchase shares directly from the company provide an inexpensive source of financing. The proceeds often are used for general corporate purposes. From the point of view of investors, however, newly issued stock dilutes existing shares, which can have the effect of depressing share prices.

The plan prospectus or description specifies when shares are purchased by the agent. Normally, the date of purchase coincides with the dividend payment date, but some companies that permit participants to make cash investments have additional investment dates.

When shares are purchased in the open markets, most plans give some discretion on buying to the agent because a large purchase made on a single date could affect the share price. Usually, the plan requires that all moneys be invested within 30 days. The share price for any participant is an average price of all shares purchased for that investment period.

The prospectus or plan description describes how the share price is determined when shares are purchased directly from the company. Generally, it is based on an average of the high and low or the closing price for the stock as reported by a specified source.

Discounts on the share price sometimes are offered to participants in company plans but with wide variations. In most cases, discounts are available only on shares purchased with reinvested dividends. But some companies permit discounts on shares purchased both with reinvested dividends and with cash payments. A few companies offer discounts only on newly issued corporate shares and not on shares that are bought in the secondary markets.

Taxation and Reinvestment Plans

No special tax advantages are connected with reinvestment plans. A taxable event occurs whether you receive your dividends in cash or have them reinvested. If your dividends are reinvested, the IRS considers the taxable amount to be equal to the fair market value of the shares acquired with the reinvested dividends. That value is the price on the exchange or market where shares are traded, not a discounted price. In addition, any brokerage commissions paid by the company in open market purchases are considered as taxable dividend income to the participant.

At the time shares are sold, the tax basis is the fair market value as of the date the shares were acquired plus any brokerage commissions paid by the company and treated as income to the participant. If you are a DRIP member, you will receive a Form 1099-DIV each year from the company detailing dividends to be treated as income and reported to the IRS.

IN A NUTSHELL

Direct purchase plans and dividend reinvestment plans provide an added tool for long-term investors. The plans enable buy-and-hold investors to maximize long-term total return through economical direct purchases of stock and automatic reinvestment of their dividends in additional shares, effectively providing an easy-to-implement dollar cost averaging plan.

Investing in Bonds

Risks and Rewards
of Bond Investing

The bond market is huge. The U.S. government is the world's largest borrower, having more than $3 trillion of U.S. Treasury securities outstanding. The mortgage-backed securities market totals more than $4 trillion, the corporate bond market is well over $2 trillion, and more than $1.4 trillion of municipal securities are in the hands of investors. Bonds, which can be bought individually or in mutual funds, play important roles in the portfolios of millions of individual investors.

A bond is actually a negotiable IOU, or loan, an acknowledgment by the issuer that money has been borrowed and is to be repaid to the bondholder at a specified rate of interest over a predetermined period. These instruments are referred to as debt obligations as contrasted with stocks, which represent ownership of a corporation usually with the right to vote and receive dividends.

As with most loans, issuers of bonds pay interest for the temporary use of money. The amount borrowed is the principal, or face value, of the bond. The interest you receive is called the bond yield and is expressed as a percentage of the bond's face value. For example, if you pay $1,000 for a bond that pays interest of $80 a year, the bond is said to yield 8 percent ($80 divided by $1,000). Because your income from the bond generally doesn't vary from year to year, bonds are called *fixed-income securities*.

Fixed-income securities form the centerpiece of most individual investor's portfolios, and with good reason. Bonds have lower but steadier returns than stocks and represent the most reliable source of income. In addition, when added to a portfolio of stocks, bonds act as stabilizers because they reduce the volatility of your overall returns. And even though bonds also will reduce the growth potential of your portfolio below that of stocks alone, the real advantage of stock-bond diversification is that it lowers your risk more than it lowers your potential return.

Some affluent investors use municipal bonds as a source of tax-exempt interest income. Because municipal bonds tend to have lower before-tax interest yields than those on taxable bonds, this investment is usually appropriate only for people in high tax brackets. (See Chapter 24 for more on the benefits of tax-free bonds.)

Investors sometimes use short-term, high-quality bonds as an alternative to money market funds. This strategy can provide higher returns, but it does entail the risk that you could lose some principal because of fluctuating bond prices.

The success of your long-term financial plan depends to a large degree on how you allocate your assets, striking the right balance between bonds, stocks, and cash reserves.

Types of Bonds

Bonds can have considerable variations in maturity, and they may have a wide range of credit ratings. Bonds are issued by the federal government and its agencies, state and local governments, and corporations.

U.S. Treasury securities come in three forms:

1. *U.S. Treasury bills,* which have maturities ranging from 90 days to 1 year
2. *U.S. Treasury notes,* which have maturities from 1 to 10 years
3. *U.S. Treasury bonds,* which have maturities from 10 to 30 years

Treasury securities are considered the safest of all debt instruments because they are legally backed by the full faith and credit of the U.S. government. This designation, which is the highest level of backing given on a U.S. government security, means that the government pledges to use its full taxing and borrowing authority, as well as revenue from nontax sources, to pay interest and repay the face amount of the security. Nonetheless, the market prices of these securities are not guaranteed and will fluctuate daily—just like the prices of any other bonds. Interest paid on Treasury bonds usually is exempt from state and local income taxes but not from federal income taxes.

U.S. Government Agency Bonds

U.S. government agency bonds and securities are issued by agencies that are owned, backed, or sponsored by the U.S. government. Although some of those bonds and securities are backed by the full faith and credit of the government, others carry less formal guarantees. The most common agency securities are mortgage pass-through securities such as those issued by the Government National Mortgage Association (Ginnie Mae), the Federal National Mortgage Association (Fannie Mae), and the Federal Home Loan Mortgage Corporation (Freddie Mac). Mortgage pass-through securities are backed by home mortgage loans.

By purchasing mortgage pass-through securities, investors are making mortgage loans to homeowners through intermediary companies. Homeowners make monthly mortgage payments to mortgage-servicing companies, and those payments flow through to investors holding the mortgage pass-through security. Of these agencies, only Ginnie Mae offers securities that are backed by the full faith and credit of the U.S. government. Nonetheless, bond market professionals believe that all of these securities have a very high credit quality, meaning that the issuing agency is very likely to pay the bond's interest and principal in full and on time. These agency securities are regarded as equal or even superior to bonds issued by the most creditworthy corporate borrowers. Other U.S. government agencies also issue securities, and you should carefully investigate the level of backing provided by the U.S. Treasury for those investments.

Corporate Bonds

Corporate bonds are issued by companies of varying quality and in various maturities—from short-term (between one and five years) and intermediate-term (between five and ten years) to long-term (more than ten years). Most corporate bonds are assigned a letter-coded rating by independent bond rating agencies such as Moody's Investors Service, and Standard & Poor's Corporation to indicate their relative credit quality—the likelihood that the issuer will pay interest and principal in full and on time. Investment-grade bonds are issued by well-regarded companies and rated as desirable investments. To be considered investment-grade, a bond must be rated BBB or better by Standard & Poor's or Baa or better by Moody's. Corporate bonds with a lower rating or no rating are sometimes called high-yield bonds because of the higher interest rates they must pay to attract investors. They are also sometimes referred to as junk bonds because the issuers are believed more likely to default—that is, fail to make full interest and principal payments as scheduled.

Municipal Bonds

Municipal bonds are issued by state and local governments to support their financial needs or to finance public projects. Interest paid on municipal bonds is typically exempt from federal income taxes and, in some cases, from state and local taxes too. However, capital gains earned on a municipal bond investment—like capital gains on any security—are subject to federal and, possibly, state and local income taxes as well. Like corporate bonds, municipal bonds come with a variety of ratings to reflect the fact that some state and local governments are financially stronger than others. Municipal bonds have maturities ranging from less than 1 year to 40 years and also are known as tax-exempt, or tax-free, bonds.

Investing in Individual Bonds

Bonds can be purchased individually or in bond funds. You may decide to purchase individual bonds for a number of reasons. First, you may have great confidence in the ability of the bond issuer to make all interest payments as promised and to repay the principal in full at maturity. By holding individual bonds, you choose when to buy or sell—thus retaining control over the timing of any taxable capital gains or losses. Moreover, you don't pay any fees for professional management or recordkeeping and so are able to receive all the income produced by the bonds before any applicable taxes. Finally, you may want assurance that the value of the investment will be paid in full on a certain date so it can be targeted to pay for an expected cost, such as a college tuition bill. Because a bond's interest rate is known, you can predict the value of the investment at maturity. For instance, if you purchase for $1,000 a bond today that pays 5 percent interest and matures in one year, you'll receive $50 in interest and $1,000 in principal in the next year for a total value of $1,050.

Keep in mind that you must pay brokerage commissions when you buy or sell individual bonds. One exception is that you may purchase U.S. Treasury securities without paying commissions through the TreasuryDirect program (www.treasurydirect.org) of the Federal Reserve System. (See Chapter 25 for more on TreasuryDirect.)

How Returns Are Calculated

The total return of a bond is the change in value of your investment over a particular period, assuming that all interest payments have been reinvested. Two components added together determine a bond's total return:

1. *Yield (interest income).* When you purchase for $1,000 a bond paying $80 interest, for example, you can expect to receive an annualized yield of 8 percent, the bond's interest income reflected as a percentage of the purchase price.
2. *Capital return.* Yield or interest income is not the only way of determining how profitable your investment has been. Although the issuer of a bond promises to pay its face value at maturity, the value of your bond may fluctuate between the issue date and maturity date, usually because of an upward or downward movement in interest rates. Thus, a $1,000 bond coming due in the year 2010 may today be worth $900 or $1,000, depending on whether interest rates in general are higher or lower than the rate paid by your bond. This rise or fall in the value of your principal is the capital return.

If a $1,000 bond drops in price to $950, your capital return would be a loss of 5 percent. Combine that with the bond's 8 percent yield and your total return becomes approximately 3 percent (8 percent yield minus 5 percent capital loss).

Factors Affecting Total Return

- *Interest rates.* The first factor that can affect the total return you receive on your fixed-income investment is a change that may take place in interest rates. Generally the market value of bonds moves in the opposite direction from interest rates. So the value of your bonds declines if interest rates go up, and it rises if interest rates

FIGURE 22.1 / EFFECT OF INTEREST RATE CHANGES ON BOND PRICES

| | INITIAL PRINCIPAL OF $1,000 AND YIELD OF 10% | | | |
| | 1% RISE IN RATES | | 1% DECLINE IN RATES | |
BOND MATURITY	PRICE	% CHANGE	PRICE	%CHANGE
Short-term (2.5 years)	$979	−2.1%	$1,022	+2.2%
Intermediate-term (7 years)	952	−4.8	1,051	+5.1
Long-term (20 years)	920	−8.0	1,092	+9.2

go down. For example, suppose you own a $1,000 face amount bond that pays 8 percent ($80 per year) and you want to sell it. But you find that similar bonds of the same quality and maturity are now paying 9 percent. To sell, your bond would have to be priced at an amount that would provide a prospective buyer with a 9 percent yield. Thus, you would be able to sell it for approximately $889, because the annual interest of $80 on a bond with a cost of $889 provides a yield of 9 percent ($80 divided by $889).

- *Maturity.* A bond's maturity also affects how much its value is apt to rise or fall. Bonds with longer maturities usually offer higher yields but also tend to have more volatile price swings than those with shorter maturities. The longer the life of a bond (its maturity), the greater the degree of its price fluctuation. Consequently, more cautious investors typically prefer shorter-term bonds because their exposure to volatility is much less.

  Figure 22.1 shows how the prices of bonds with varying maturities would respond following a 1 percent change in interest rates. As you can see, rising interest rates result in decreasing bond values and vice versa. Further, the degree of volatility increases as maturities lengthen. Note how much more volatility affects the values of long-term bonds than those of intermediate-term or short-term bonds.

- *Credit quality.* Although interest rates and maturity can influence the face value of a bond, a bond's credit quality has an important bearing on its yield. Credit risk is the chance that your bond will default (fail to make timely payment of principal and interest). Lower-quality bonds usually offer higher yields but also have a greater risk of default.

FIGURE 22.2 / BOND-QUALITY RATINGS

Moody's Investors Service	Standard & Poor's Corporation	
Aaa	AAA	Judged to be the best quality, carrying the smallest degree of credit risk. U.S. government and U.S. agency bonds have Aaa and AAA ratings.
Aa	AA	Regarded as high quality. Together with Aaa and AAA bonds, they are known as high-grade bonds.
A	A	Possess many favorable investment attributes and are considered to be high medium-grade bonds.
Baa	BBB	Considered medium-grade—neither highly protected nor poorly secured.
Ba	BB	Judged to have speculative elements. Their futures cannot be considered well ensured.
B	B	Generally lack characteristics of a desirable investment.
Caa	CCC	Considered poor quality with danger of default.
Ca	CC	Regarded as very speculative quality, often in default.
C	C	Lowest rating; considered to have poor prospects of repayment though the bond may still be paying.
D	D	In default.

Note: Moody's applies numerical modifiers (1, 2, and 3) in each rating classification from Aa through Baa in its corporate bond rating system. The modifier 1 indicates that the bond ranks in the higher end of its category, 2 indicates a midrange ranking, and 3 indicates a low ranking.

The Standard & Poor's ratings from AA to CCC may be modified by a plus sign (+) or a minus sign (−) to indicate relative standing within the major rating categories.

The credit quality of a bond depends on the issuer's ability to pay interest on the bond and ultimately to repay the principal at maturity. Independent bond rating agencies evaluate the financial health of bond issuers and issue alphabetical credit-quality ratings. Usually a lower credit rating means that the issuer must pay higher interest to offset the higher risk that principal and interest won't be repaid on time. Figure 22.2 describes the ratings used by Moody's Investor Service and Standard & Poor's Corporation.

Just as interest rates and bond values have an inverse relationship, the creditworthiness of an issuer and the interest paid have a similar relationship. For instance, the safest investment you can make, guaranteed by the full faith and credit of the U.S. government as to the timely payment of principal and interest, usually pays a lower interest rate. As you move down the scale to less creditworthy and therefore more speculative bonds, the issuer is forced to pay a higher interest rate to compensate for the greater risk.

IN A NUTSHELL

Bonds generally produce a higher and steadier flow of income than you would receive from money market funds or bank savings accounts, and the amount invested is usually at less risk than if you had invested it in stocks. Before investing in bonds, though, assess the bonds' market and credit risk to determine whether they are compatible with your personal risk tolerance level.

CHAPTER 23

Bond Mutual Funds

Despite the significant advantages of purchasing individual bonds, identifying and managing appropriate ones for investment is a time-consuming process that requires a fairly high level of expertise. As a result, many investors have found that a smart way to buy bonds is through bond mutual funds, available through investment brokers, banks, and often directly from fund companies. This approach typically results in a higher total return on your investment with less risk.

Americans have invested more than $850 billion in bond funds, according to the Investment Company Institute (www.ici.org). Like all mutual funds, a bond fund pools money from many investors and uses the money to buy securities that meet the fund's stated investment objectives and policies. The decisions to buy and sell individual bonds are made by a professional portfolio manager.

A bond fund offers the following important advantages to investors:

- *Regular monthly income.* A typical bond fund distributes virtually all of its interest income as a dividend distribution each month. You may choose to receive these dividends as cash or to have them automatically reinvested. Individual bonds generally pay interest at six-month intervals, and those payments cannot automatically be reinvested.
- *Lower investment amounts.* The minimum amount for an individual bond investment can be as high as $10,000. In contrast, the

minimum initial investment in a bond fund is often considerably lower, so an investor with limited funds still can participate in the bond market. A mutual fund investor also can purchase additional fund shares in amounts far smaller than the cost of an individual bond.

- *Diversification.* A bond fund may hold bonds from hundreds of different issuers, meaning that it offers diversification. In a diversified fund, the failure of one issuer to pay interest or principal has only a slight effect on investors, whereas the owners of individual bonds could lose most or all of their investment if an issuer defaults.
- *Professional investment management.* A professional investment manager—who has access to extensive research, market information, and skilled securities traders—decides which securities to buy and sell for a bond fund. Professional management can be a valuable service because few investors have the time or expertise to manage their personal investments on a daily basis or to investigate the thousands of bonds available in the financial markets.
- *Daily liquidity.* Shares in a bond mutual fund may be bought or sold whenever you choose; in other words, the fund offers liquidity. In addition, most bond funds offer such options as checkwriting and telephone redemption to make bond investing more convenient. These benefits are generally not available to owners of individual bonds because most bonds cost hundreds or thousands of dollars each and must be traded through a brokerage account.

In addition to its advantages, a bond fund also has some potential disadvantages:

- The dividend income paid by a bond fund is not fixed as it is with an individual bond. As a result, the actual dividend the investor receives may go up or down slightly as the fund buys and sells individual bonds.
- A bond fund has no maturity date. Instead, a fund maintains an average rolling maturity by selling off aging bonds and buying newer ones—which could create unwanted taxable capital gains for the fund's shareholders. After five years, a five-year bond fund will still have a five-year average maturity, but a five-year bond would have matured and been paid off.
- The owner of an individual bond has the option of holding the investment to maturity and receiving the face amount of the bond. A bond fund investor, however, may have to redeem the

investment at a price higher or lower than the original purchase price—thus realizing a capital gain or loss.

Investment Returns on Bond Funds

Every mutual fund has a net asset value (NAV), the share price that reflects the value of a fund's total net assets divided by the number of shares outstanding. The NAV fluctuates daily as the prices of the fund's investments change. When you invest in a bond fund, the price per share that you pay is the NAV at the close of the trade date. Similarly, when you sell (redeem) existing shares, the price per share is again the closing NAV.

A mutual fund's investment performance is best measured by its total return—the percentage change in its value over a specific period, including any change in the fund's share price as well as any reinvested income or capital gains. Thus, the total return of a bond fund has two components:

- *Income return.* A bond fund's interest income expressed as a percentage of net asset value is called its income return, or yield. If you are relying on the fund for income, this component of the total return is the most important. In simple terms, a $1,000 investment in a bond fund that pays $70 a year in dividend income provides a 7 percent income return (yield).
- *Capital return.* A measure of the increase or decrease in the fund's net asset value is called its capital return. If the value of a bond fund investment falls from $1,000 to $980, the capital return would be –2 percent. If income is not the main reason for investing in a bond fund, this component is more important.

Total return is the sum of income return and capital return. Thus, an investment with a 7 percent annual income return and a –2 percent annual capital return has a total return of 5 percent for the year. Income return will never be negative, but total return could be negative because of capital losses.

How Expenses Affect Return

Regardless of the type of mutual fund, you should pay close attention to fees and expenses, for they directly reduce a fund's total return. Those costs are particularly important to bond fund investors because they are the most important difference between comparable bond funds. Once you have chosen a level of credit quality (for instance, Treasury versus corporate securities) and an average maturity, most funds will have a similar gross yield—the yield before expenses. Because investors receive only the net yield—the yield after expenses—high expenses can consume a substantial amount of a bond fund's yield.

If you own a short-term corporate bond fund with a gross yield of 6.5 percent and an expense ratio of 0.86 percent (the average expense ratio for short-term investment-grade corporate bond funds in 1998), for example, its net yield to you will be only 5.64 percent. If a similar fund has the same gross yield but an expense ratio of 0.28 percent (the 1998 expense ratio for Vanguard Short-Term Corporate Fund), the net yield to you would be 6.22 percent. The interest income you receive in the low-cost fund would be 10 percent greater than the interest income you'd receive in the higher-cost fund. You should be aware that a manager of a high-cost fund may be tempted to overcome this performance disadvantage by taking on additional risk in the hope of receiving higher returns. Conversely, the manager of a low-cost fund may be able to provide competitive returns with a lower level of risk than other funds.

Effect of Sales Charges (Loads)

Investors in some mutual funds also may have to pay sales charges, or front-end loads, when they invest—and those charges can take up to 8.5 percent of the initial investment. Another sales charge is a back-end load that can take up to 6 percent of an investment when it is redeemed—although the charges usually decline the longer an investment is held. Finally, some funds charge 12b-1 fees, which are used to pay marketing and distribution costs of the funds. This can be as much as 1 percent of assets, or $10 a year for each $1,000 invested. Funds that have no sales charges are called no-load funds, while funds that have neither sales loads nor 12b-1 fees are called pure no-load funds. Figure 23.1 shows how fees and expenses can vary considerably from one fund to another. Look for funds with low expenses, such as those offered by The Vanguard Group (www.vanguard.com) and USAA (www.usa.com/cp_aboutusaa.asp).

FIGURE 23.1 / SALES COMMISSIONS AND EXPENSES FOR TAXABLE BOND FUNDS

BOND FUNDS	SALES COMMISSION	ANNUAL EXPENSE RATIO	ANNUAL 12b-1 FEE	TOTAL FUND EXPENSES
USAA GNMA Trust	None	0.32%	None	0.32%
Vanguard Long-Term Corporate Fund	None	0.32	None	0.32
Pure no-load funds*	None	0.82	None	0.82
No-load funds (with 12b-1 fees)*	None	0.83	0.17	1.00
Front-end load funds (without 12b-1 fees)*	3.79%	0.90	None	4.69
Front-end load funds (with 12b-1 fees)*	3.97	1.04	0.25	5.26
Load funds (front-end or back-end with 12b-1 fees)*	3.95	1.33	0.54	5.82

---

*Industry average

Bond Fund Risks

Bond funds are subject to a variety of risks. Unlike bank deposits or money market funds, the value of a bond fund goes up and down. When a rapid rise in interest rates in 1994 caused long-term bond funds to lose 8 percent of their value, investors learned that bond funds can sometimes be as risky as stock funds.

Before investing in any bond fund, you should consider these risks:

- *Interest rate risk.* Bond funds decrease in value when interest rates rise, and they increase in value when rates fall. The risk that a bond fund will rise or fall in value is known as interest rate risk, and the longer a bond fund's maturity or duration, the greater the interest rate risk. You can reduce   but not eliminate   interest rate risk by concentrating on short-term and intermediate-term bond funds.
- *Income risk.* In periods of declining market interest rates, a bond fund's interest income may fall, so an investor seeking current in-

come could see that income reduced when interest rates decline. Income risk is higher for short-term bond funds and lower for long-term funds because short-term funds hold bonds for a shorter period of time than do long-term funds. As interest rates change, short-term bonds mature and those assets must be reinvested at the new higher or lower interest rates.

- *Call risk.* The term *call risk* refers to the possibility that some bonds can be called (redeemed by the issuer before they mature) when the issuer believes that doing so would be economically advantageous. This usually occurs when interest rates fall below the rate specified on the bond. When a bond is called, the bondholders must then reinvest their money—often at a lower yield. A similar risk—prepayment risk—affects mortgage-backed securities such as Ginnie Maes (Government National Mortgage Association securities). When interest rates fall, many homeowners pay off their mortgages by refinancing, so the securities backing those mortgages also must be paid off.

- *Credit risk.* Bond investors can lose money if an issuer defaults or if a bond's credit rating is reduced. Because a mutual fund invests in many bonds, the possibility that a single default would significantly hurt investors is reduced. Credit risk is typically lowest with U.S. Treasury bonds, followed by U.S. government agency bonds, then by corporate and municipal bonds that have high ratings. Investors in high-yield bonds or bond funds are subject to greater credit risks, especially in an economic downturn.

- *Inflation risk.* A bond investment can lose purchasing power as prices rise—so inflation risk is a serious concern for anyone relying on the income to pay for future needs. If inflation ran at 3 percent for five years, for example, the value of a $100 payment check would be reduced to $86 in terms of actual purchasing power. In the long run, inflation can have a dramatic effect on the value of bonds, which typically include no potential for growth.

- *Manager risk.* Many bond funds are actively managed, meaning that the portfolio manager uses economic, financial, and market analyses when deciding which bonds to buy or sell. Manger risk refers to the possibility that the portfolio manager may fail to choose an effective investment strategy or to execute that strategy well. As a result, an investor in the fund may lose money.

- *Other risks.* Some bond funds may also be exposed to event risk, the possibility that some corporate bonds may suffer a substantial decline in credit quality and market value because of a corporate restructuring—for example, a merger, leveraged buyout, or take-over. Restructurings are sometimes financed by a significant increase in the company's debt—an added burden that could hurt the credit quality of the company's existing bonds. Still more risks can arise from the use of derivatives, such as futures or options, whose values are linked to (or derived from) the value of another asset or commodity. Because different derivative-trading strategies carry different amounts of potential risk and reward, some funds limit the use of derivatives by their portfolio managers.

Choosing the Right Bond Fund

Once you have decided to invest in bond funds, the next step is to choose the types of funds in which to invest. Before choosing a bond fund, you should consider the following questions:

- *What degree of risk is acceptable?* The amount of risk you can assume will dictate whether you invest in a short-, intermediate-, or long-term bond fund. If you're worried about bond market fluctuations, consider funds with lower average maturities and durations because those funds have lower price volatility than long-term funds. If you have a long time horizon and are seeking higher returns, you'll be more likely to choose a long-term bond fund.
- *What is important—credit quality or yield?* An investor seeking the highest investment quality will consider U.S. government bond funds; an investor who prefers higher yields might prefer corporate bond funds. In making this decision, you should remember that most bond funds are broadly diversified, so the added credit risk associated with the typical corporate bond fund is relatively modest.
- *Are you in a high tax bracket?* If your investment is being made outside a tax-deferred retirement plan and you are in a high tax bracket, you may want to investigate tax-exempt bond funds rather than taxable bond funds.
- *How much income do you need?* The amount of income you need from a bond investment will influence the degree of risk that you accept. If more income is needed, you could choose a bond fund with a longer average maturity—and so take on more market risk. Or you could decide to invest in a fund with lower-rated securities. If less income is needed, then you can invest in a fund with higher-rated securities and/or a shorter average maturity.

IN A NUTSHELL

You are likely to achieve a higher total return on your fixed-income investments, with less risk, by purchasing bond mutual funds. This investment choice gives you the advantages of diversification, professional management, low cost, monthly income, and liquidity. Plus you're not faced with the problem of reinvesting the proceeds of individual bonds as they mature.

Tax-Free Income from Municipal Bonds

Most investors carefully evaluate yield, safety, and growth potential when they choose an investment. Yet few stop to consider the effect of taxes on their investment return. An investor in the 36 percent tax bracket, for example, could be giving up $36 of every $100 of investment income to taxes. From a different perspective, an 8 percent income return equals just 5.12 percent after taxes.

Income from municipal bonds is exempt from federal income taxes and, in some cases, from state and local taxes as well. However, municipal bonds (which pay lower yields than taxable bonds as the trade-off for their tax advantage) are not for everyone. Generally, investors in the 15 or 28 percent tax bracket don't benefit from owning municipal bonds.

Municipal bonds, often called *munis* or *tax-exempts,* appeal to investors for two reasons:

1. *Tax-free income.* Municipal bonds are one of the few remaining sources of tax-free income. They provide income that is exempt from federal income taxes and often are free from state and local taxes in the state of issue. The state of New York, for instance, might issue a bond to help pay for repaving a tollway, then use the money collected from the tolls to repay investors. The interest income from this bond would be exempt from federal income taxes, and for New York residents the interest also would be exempt from state and city taxes.

Income from some municipal bonds is subject to the federal alternative minimum tax (AMT), which applies to certain high-income investors. Such investors should check to see if a bond they are considering is subject to AMT before investing.

2. *Diversification.* Bonds have investment characteristics different from those of common stocks. Though bond prices are sometimes quite volatile, they are generally considered safer than stocks and can serve to diversify an equity-heavy portfolio. Municipal bonds are generally considered to be high on the investment safety scale, second only to securities issued by the U.S. government and its agencies.

Tax-free investments have been gaining in popularity. According to *Bond Buyer* magazine, more than 75 percent of municipal obligations are owned by individuals through their investments in individual bonds and mutual funds. With more than $1.25 trillion of municipal debt outstanding, the sheer size of the tax-free bond market helps to make it stable and liquid, so buying and selling bonds is relatively easy.

What Are Municipal Bonds?

Municipal bonds are interest-bearing securities issued by state and local governments to support their financial needs or to finance public projects. A municipal bond obligates the issuer to pay the bondholder a fixed amount of interest periodically and to repay the principal value of the bond on a specified maturity date. Like bonds issued by corporations or the U.S. government, municipal bonds are considered fixed-income securities because they offer a steady rate of interest income. They often are called *debt obligations,* as they represent a loan to the bond issuer. There are two basic types of municipal bonds:

1. *General obligation (GO) bonds.* GO bonds are issued by municipal agencies, such as cities or states, that have taxing authority. Payments of principal and interest on GO bonds are secured by the full faith and credit of the issuer. Thus, the issuing agency promises to use every means available to ensure prompt payment of principal and interest when they're due.

2. *Revenue bonds.* Revenue bonds are payable from a specific source of income. Sources of income frequently used to pay the interest on revenue bond issues include tolls and rents or charges from such facilities as turnpikes, airports, hospitals, and water treatment plants.

FIGURE 24.1 / CONVERSION TABLE FOR TAX-EXEMPT AND TAXABLE BONDS

EQUIVALENT TAX-EXEMPT YIELDS
FOR TAXABLE BONDS
YIELD ON TAXABLE BOND

MARGINAL TAX BRACKET	5.0%	5.5%	6.0%	6.5%	7.0%	7.5%	8.0%
15.0%	4.3%	5.7%	5.1%	5.5%	6.0%	6.4%	6.8%
28.0	3.6	4.0	4.3	4.7	5.0	5.4	5.8
31.0	3.5	3.8	4.1	4.5	4.8	5.2	5.5
36.0	3.2	3.5	3.8	4.2	4.5	4.8	5.1
39.6	3.0	3.3	3.6	3.9	4.2	4.5	4.8

TAXABLE EQUIVALENT YIELDS
FOR TAX-EXEMPT BONDS
YIELD ON TAX-EXEMPT BOND

MARGINAL TAX BRACKET	3.5%	4.0%	4.5%	5.0%	5.5%	6.0%	6.5%
15.0%	4.1%	4.7%	5.3%	5.9%	6.5%	7.1%	7.6%
28.0	4.9	5.6	6.3	6.9	7.6	8.3	9.0
31.0	5.1	5.8	6.5	7.2	8.0	8.7	9.4
36.0	5.5	6.3	7.0	7.8	8.6	9.4	10.2
39.6	5.8	6.6	7.5	8.3	9.1	9.9	10.8

Tax-Exempt versus Taxable Bonds

Deciding between tax-exempt and taxable bonds for your portfolio takes some analysis. Municipal bonds offer the advantage of producing income that is exempt from taxes—but they also pay yields lower than those available on taxable bonds of comparable quality and maturity. To decide whether to invest in tax-exempt bonds or taxable ones, you need to know which provide the best overall return.

Here's how to compare the yield of a tax-exempt municipal bond with that of a taxable bond that is of similar credit quality and maturity. First subtract the percentage of your marginal tax bracket from one, then divide the resulting number into the yield of the tax-exempt bond to find the equivalent taxable yield. For an investor in the 28 percent tax bracket considering a tax-exempt bond with a yield of 6 percent, the calculation is as follows:

Example: $1.00 - 0.28 = 0.72$
$6\% \div 0.72 = 8.33\%$

In this example, a taxable fund must provide a yield of more than 8.33 percent to top a yield of 6 percent from a tax-exempt fund. Generally, if you are in the 31 percent tax bracket or higher, municipal bonds will suit you better than taxable bonds. Figure 24.1 shows equivalent tax-exempt yields for taxable bonds, as well as equivalent taxable yields for tax-exempt bonds.

Municipal Bond Investment Risks

As is true with corporate bonds, interest rate risk and credit risk are two major factors you should assess before investing in a municipal bond.

When Orange County, California, filed for bankruptcy in late 1994, it sent shock waves through the investment community. Orange County was the biggest U.S. municipality ever to take that action. One way municipal bond investors can protect themselves from the risk of default is by purchasing AAA (triple A) rated insured municipal bonds. The higher credit quality, of course, means you will earn a slightly lower yield. Holders of insured bonds are guaranteed they will continue to receive principal and interest payments on time and in full if their bonds default. Although uninsured Orange County bonds were downgraded after the county's financial problems became known, its AAA insured bonds were not.

Even though less than 1 percent of local government bonds default, demand for insurance is great enough that half of all new-issue municipal bonds are insured, giving them a triple A rating. Each guarantee is unconditional and irrevocable and covers 100 percent of interest and principal for the full term of the issue. Aside from the protection against default, many investors choose insured bonds because the extra protection and triple A rating insulates them from the uncertainty that sometimes depresses prices and makes it difficult to sell bonds that are involved in controversy even though they have not defaulted.

Major insurers of municipal bonds—all members of the Association of Financial Guaranty Insurors (AFGI) (www.afgi.org)—include

AMBAC Indemnity Corporation, Capital Guaranty Insurance Company, Financial Guaranty Insurance Company, Financial Security Assurance, and Municipal Bond Investors Assurance Corporation. Each of these companies' claims-paying ability is rated triple A by one or more of the major rating agencies. In the 28 years of the bond insurance industry, no investor in a bond insured by an AFGI member company has ever failed to receive a bond payment, and no AFGI-insured bond has ever been downgraded from triple A.

Issuers often prefer to offer their bonds with insurance to lower borrowing costs. By boosting the rating on a security, bond insurance enables the issuer to save on interest costs because bonds with the highest rating—and thus with the greatest security—pay the least interest. Bond insurance is cost effective for an issuer so long as the interest cost savings exceed the premium paid to the insurer. Since the inception of municipal bond insurance in 1971, municipalities have saved approximately $20 billion in borrowing costs through bond insurance.

IN A NUTSHELL

Municipal bonds can provide one of the few remaining sources of tax-free income. The interest they pay is exempt from federal income taxes and in some cases is exempt from state and local taxes. Taxpayers in the highest marginal tax brackets (above 28 percent) benefit most from municipal bonds.

Buying U.S. Treasury Securities through TreasuryDirect

It's a lot easier than you think to buy U.S. Treasury securities, the safest investments money can buy, without paying any commissions, fees, or other charges through a system called TreasuryDirect. These securities are direct obligations of the U.S. government. And Treasury-Direct lets you buy Treasury bills (T-bills), T-notes, and T-bonds directly from the government—without brokers, without hassles, and without a mountain of paperwork.

You can use the phone (800-943-6864) or the Internet (www.trea surydirect.gov) to make your TreasuryDirect purchase and perform many of the functions needed to maintain your account. Or if you prefer, you may choose the more traditional paper forms.

The U.S. Treasury issues three types of marketable securities: bills, notes, and bonds. When originally issued, Treasuries are sold through an auction process. They are referred to as marketable securities because after their original issue, they are bought and sold in the secondary (commercial) market at prevailing market prices through financial institutions, brokers, and dealers in investment securities. Marketable Treasury securities are issued only in book-entry form at original issue. Book-entry securities are represented by accounting entries maintained electronically on the records of the U.S. Treasury, a Federal Reserve Bank or branch, or a financial institution. Certificates are no longer offered at original issue.

TreasuryDirect

If you elect to invest in T-bills, T-notes, or T-bonds by using the TreasuryDirect book-entry system, you may purchase securities at original issue through any Federal Reserve Bank or branch. For each purchaser of marketable Treasury securities in TreasuryDirect, the Treasury Department establishes an investor account. Actually, you automatically request that an investor account be established when you complete a tender form. Once an account is established, it serves as a single account for all of your marketable Treasury securities eligible to be maintained in TreasuryDirect. Different registrations and account information require establishment of separate TreasuryDirect accounts. Principal and interest payments from a TreasuryDirect account are paid electronically by direct deposit into your account in a locally authorized bank or other financial institution.

The TreasuryDirect system is designed primarily for investors who plan to retain their securities from the issue date to maturity. However, you may arrange through a bank or brokerage firm for your investment to be sold before maturity. This is done by requesting that your securities held in the TreasuryDirect system be transferred to the commercial system. Your request must be made at least 20 days before an interest payment date or the maturity date of the security.

The Federal Reserve System has set up 37 Servicing Offices to assist you with your TreasuryDirect questions. You easily can find the Servicing Office for your area by entering your zip code once you have accessed the TreasuryDirect system's Web site (www.treasurydirect. gov).

Offering Schedule of Treasury Securities

Following is the general pattern of financing for marketable T-bills, T-notes, and T-bonds. The Treasury's borrowing requirements, financing policy decisions, and the timing of congressional action on the debt limit could alter or delay the pattern.

Treasury Bills

- Thirteen-week and 26-week bills are offered each week. Except for holidays or special circumstances (1) the offering is announced on Thursday, (2) the bills are auctioned the following Tuesday, and (3) they are issued on the Thursday following the auction.

- Fifty-two-week bills are offered every four weeks. Except for holidays or special circumstances (1) the offering is announced every fourth Thursday, (2) the bills are auctioned the following Tuesday, and (3) they are issued on the Thursday following the auction.
- Cash management bills are offered from time to time depending on borrowing needs. The time between announcement, auction, and issue is usually short (one to seven days).

Treasury Notes and Bonds

- Two-year notes are issued once a month. The notes are generally announced near the middle of each month and auctioned one week later. They usually are issued on the last day of each month; if the last day of the month is a Saturday, Sunday, or federal holiday, however, the notes are issued on the first business day of the following month.
- Five-year note auctions are usually announced on the first Wednesday of February, May, August, and November. They generally are auctioned during the second week of February, May, August, and November and are issued on the 15th of the same month. If the 15th falls on a Saturday, Sunday, or federal holiday, the securities are issued on the next business day.
- Ten-year note auctions are usually announced on the first Wednesday of February, May, August, and November. They generally are auctioned during the second week of February, May, August, and November, and are issued on the 15th of the same month. If the 15th falls on a Saturday, Sunday, or federal holiday, the securities are issued on the next business day.
- Inflation-indexed security (note or bond) auctions are usually announced on the first Wednesday of January, April, July, and October. They generally are auctioned during the second week of January, April, July, and October, and are issued on the 15th of the same month. If the 15th falls on a Saturday, Sunday, or federal holiday, the securities are issued on the next business day.
- Thirty-year bond auctions usually are announced along with five-year and ten-year notes on the first Wednesday of February, August, and November. They generally are auctioned during the second week of those months and issued on the 15th. If the 15th falls on a Saturday, Sunday, or federal holiday, the securities are issued the next business day.

How to Buy Treasury Securities

Once the Department of the Treasury announces an auction, investors are invited to submit bids. Depending on the type of bid, you can submit your offer over the Internet, by phone, or by paper form. For all Treasury securities—bills, notes, and bonds—the minimum purchase amount is $1,000; and bids must be made in multiples of $1,000. Noncompetitive bids from a single bidder may not exceed $1 million for the same offering of Treasury bills, or $5 million for the same offering of Treasury notes or bonds.

The two types of bids are:

1. *Noncompetitive bid.* The investor agrees to accept a rate determined by the auction and in return is guaranteed a security. Most individual investors choose this type of bid, which can be made over the Internet, by phone, or by paper form.

2. *Competitive bid.* The investor submits a tender specifying a discount rate with three decimal places in increments of .005 percent (e.g., 7.100%, 7.105%) for a bill auction or specifying a yield to three decimal places for a note or bond auction (e.g., 7.123%). Cash management bills are expressed as a discount rate with two decimals (e.g., 7.10%). Common fractions may not be used. If the bid falls within the range accepted at auction, the investor will be awarded the security. If the bid is at the high rate or yield, the investor may not be awarded the full amount bid. Competitive bids must be submitted by paper form; and competitive bidders may have their bids rejected.

Investors who want to bid competitively in an auction should contact a Federal Reserve Bank Servicing Office or the Bureau of the Public Debt's Capital Area Servicing Center for further information. Information may be obtained over the Internet at www.treasurydirect.gov.

Paper tender forms and payments may be mailed directly to your nearest Federal Reserve Bank Servicing Office or the Bureau of the Public Debt's Capital Area Servicing Center. Tenders must be received by the time stated in the offering announcement. Generally, the deadlines are by 12 NOON Eastern time on the auction day for hand-delivered noncompetitive bids and by 1:00 PM Eastern time on the auction day for competitive bids. Noncompetitive bids that are mailed must be postmarked by the day prior to the auction and be received by the issue date of the security.

Internet and phone services enable existing TreasuryDirect accountholders to buy securities from the comfort and privacy of home. With Buy Direct, you can submit a noncompetitive bid via the Internet or by calling 800-943-6864. The price of the security is debited from the account you previously designated to receive Treasury-Direct payments.

Tender forms and payments also may be submitted electronically through your financial institution or government securities broker or dealer. These organizations generally require earlier submissions, so they have time to transmit your request for purchase to a Federal Reserve Bank or Branch by the deadline.

Reinvestment or Redemption

Securities held in TreasuryDirect are paid at maturity by direct deposit unless you have elected to reinvest the proceeds of the maturing securities into new securities.

A request for reinvestment of T-bills for a period of up to two years may be made on the tender at the time of original purchase. Reinvestment for notes and bonds held in TreasuryDirect is not available at original issue. However, owners of bills, notes, or bonds not scheduled for reinvestment are sent a preredemption notice that shows the eligible securities, if any, into which reinvestments are possible. If you wish to reinvest a security, the notice must be completed and returned by the date specified in the notice. Or, you may reinvest maturing securities by telephone or Internet at any hour of the day or night.

Taxation

Treasury securities are subject to all federal taxes, such as income, estate, gift, or excise taxes. However, interest earned on Treasury securities is exempt from state and local income taxes. The interest on bills, which are bought with the interest discounted, is taxable in the year in which the bills mature or are sold.

IN A NUTSHELL

You can invest directly over the Internet in U.S. Treasury securities without paying any commissions, fees, or other charges by setting up a TreasuryDirect account. This account will link up with your own bank or other financial institution account.

Investing in Mutual Funds

Mutual Funds: America's Most Popular Investment Medium

In early 1999, some 7,000 mutual funds were entrusted by investors with more than $5.5 trillion, according to the Investment Company Institute (www.ici.org). At an increasingly rapid pace, mutual funds have come to have an important and in some ways dominant place in the financial world. They have become the investment of choice for millions of investors and with good reason.

Although their popularity has mushroomed in recent years, mutual funds have been around for a long time. The oldest mutual funds in existence are more than 70 years old, having survived the Great Depression, World War II, and other turbulent economic and political events.

In a somewhat different form, the origin of modern day mutual funds dates back to the early 19th century, when they enjoyed substantial popularity in England and Scotland. In the 1820s, the so-called mutuals reached the United States in the form of a vehicle created by Massachusetts Hospital Life Insurance. Generally balanced between stocks and bonds, a mutual was a load fund managed by professionals and sold by commissioned agents, not unlike today's insurance agents. Many mutuals were sold through plans in which the investor might agree to a $5,000 commitment paid with $100-a-month installments. About a century later, in 1924, the Massachusetts Investment Trust was organized. It was the first open-end mutual fund and still operates as a member of the Massachusetts Financial Services group in Boston (www.mfs.com). During those early years, investment trusts were subject to various abuses and were brought into considerable disrepute. Nonetheless, by 1929 some 525,000 Americans owned shares in them.

Some of today's mutual fund giants were first organized in the 1930s. But the greatest growth of mutual funds occurred after World War II and has continued to this day with only occasional pauses. In 1946 mutual fund companies managed just over $2 billion in assets. By 1956 this had grown to $10.5 billion and to more than $39 billion in 1966. Growth became sluggish in the 1970s but then exploded in the 1980s. By 1990, 3,000 funds were managing $1 trillion in assets; the $2 trillion level was reached—and passed—in 1993 before reaching the $5.5 trillion managed today. Of this amount, about $3 trillion is in stocks with the balance in bond and money market funds.

What Is a Mutual Fund?

The idea behind a mutual fund is simple: Many people put their money in a fund, which invests in various types of securities to pursue a specific financial goal. Then, each investor shares proportionately in the income or investment gains and losses that the fund's investments produce. Because investors may sell their shares or buy new shares each business day, mutual funds are called *open-end investment companies.*

Each mutual fund has a manager, usually called a *portfolio manager,* who directs the investing of the fund's assets according to the fund's objectives. Some common objectives of mutual funds are long-term growth, high current income, stability of principal, or some combination of the three. Depending on its objective, a fund may invest in common stocks, bonds, cash investments, or a combination of these three types of financial assets.

Reasons Why Mutual Funds Are Popular

Four key attributes—diversification, professional management, liquidity, and convenience—have helped to make mutual funds America's most popular medium for investing:

1. *Diversification.* A single mutual fund may hold securities from hundreds of different issuers, a level of diversification that few investors could achieve on their own. By pooling their money,

mutual fund shareholders are able to spread their assets among many different securities, sharply reducing the risk of loss from problems with any one company or institution.

2. *Professional management.* A portfolio manager—who has access to extensive research, market information, and skilled securities traders—decides which securities to buy and sell for a mutual fund. Professional management can be a valuable service because few investors have the time or expertise to manage their personal investments on a daily basis or to investigate the thousands of securities available in the financial markets.

3. *Liquidity.* Shares in a mutual fund may be sold whenever you want. A fund is required to redeem shares each business day for the net asset value of the securities within the fund (although redemption fees apply to some funds).

4. *Convenience.* Mutual funds offer a variety of services that can make investing easier. Fund shares may be purchased or sold through the Internet, telephone, or mail, and your money easily can be moved from one fund to another as your investing needs change. You can arrange to have automatic investments made into a fund to steadily build an investment portfolio or to redeem some of your shares automatically to meet monthly living expenses. You can have distributions of fund income paid directly to you or automatically reinvested in more shares of your fund. Extensive recordkeeping services are provided to help you track your transactions, assist you in completing your tax returns, and follow your fund's performance. You can monitor the price of your fund shares daily in newspapers, by telephone, or via a variety of online services.

Disadvantages of Mutual Funds

Some disadvantages associated with investing in mutual funds are worth considering:

- *No guarantees.* Unlike bank deposits, mutual funds are not insured or guaranteed by the Federal Deposit Insurance Corporation (FDIC) or any other agency of the U.S. government. The market value of a mutual fund may fluctuate even if the fund invests in government securities. Mutual funds are regulated by the U.S. Securities and Exchange Commission (SEC) (www.sec.gov) and by state securities officials, who require funds to provide full disclosure of information an investor needs to make an informed decision. But this regulation doesn't eliminate the risk of an investment falling in value.

- *The diversification penalty.* Because a mutual fund typically holds a large number of securities, fund shareholders forgo the chance to earn the higher returns that are sometimes achieved by holding a single security or a handful of individual securities. In other words, just as diversification eliminates the risk of catastrophic loss from holding a single security, it limits the potential for a big score from holding a single stock or bond whose value shoots up. It is also important to understand that diversification doesn't protect an investor from the risk of loss from an overall decline in the financial markets.

- *Potentially high costs.* Mutual funds can be a lower-cost way to buy securities when compared with buying individual securities through a broker. However, a combination of sales commissions and high operating expenses at some funds may offset the efficiencies that can be gained through mutual fund ownership.

Mutual Fund Costs

The Investment Company Institute (ICI) (www.ici.org), the mutual fund trade association, found in a recently released study that the total shareholder cost of investing in mutual funds fell more than one-third between 1980 and 1997. The study by the ICI found that the average cost of investing in a stock fund in 1997 was 1.49 percent of each dollar invested, down from 2.25 percent in 1980.

Total shareholder costs represent the costs you incur in purchasing and holding a mutual fund, which includes fund expenses like sales commissions and management fees. The decline in shareholder costs was the result of lower distribution costs—that is, the sum of annual sales loads and 12b-1 fees. They, along with management fees and expenses, account for the costs of owning a mutual fund. Loads were substantially reduced during the period of the study as were 12b-1 fees, despite their proliferation.

The study was a rebuttal to critics of mutual fund costs, chief among them the SEC. The agency has questioned fixed fund costs in light of the explosive growth in the number of mutual funds and in their assets under management. The ICI study drew on a Lipper Analytical

Services database (www.lipperweb.com) of all mutual funds and the ICI's own data. Those data, however, were sometimes incomplete, so the ICI relied on CDA/Wiesenberger (www.wiesenberger.com), Value Line (www.valueline.com), and other sources to fill in some areas. A similar study done by Lipper, not surprisingly, had similar findings. The Lipper study said the appearance of higher expenses was due largely to the rise in new, high-expense funds, more funds charging 12b-1 fees, and higher service charges.

One of the critics that believe mutual fund costs are too high is John C. Bogle, senior chairman and founder of The Vanguard Group (www.vanguard.com), who holds that costs play a crucial role in shaping long-term fund returns and that a low expense ratio is the single most important reason why a fund does well.

The ICI and Lipper studies highlight a part of mutual fund investing that is often overlooked. Costs have an important impact on your investment results and some funds are much more costly to own than others. Once you understand fund expenses, you'll find it easier to select the most cost-effective funds.

Fund costs fall into two categories: sales charges, or loads, and operating expenses. Not all mutual funds impose loads, but all funds have ongoing operating expenses that are deducted from the income each fund earns before that income passes through to fund shareholders.

- *Sales loads.* These may be charged up front as a percentage of the sum you invest; these front-end loads range from 4 to 8.5 percent. Funds that charge sales fees ranging from 1 to 3 percent are considered low-load funds. Another form of sales charge is the back-end load, which is applied when an investor sells fund shares. Back-end loads, also known as contingent deferred sales charges, may be as high as 6 percent for a redemption that takes place within a year of the original investment. The charge typically declines over time, disappearing by the seventh year after the original purchase of fund shares.
- *Operating expenses.* All funds incur expenses from basic operations, including investment advisory fees, legal and accounting services, postage, printing, telephone service, and other costs of running the fund. These expenses are paid from income earned by the fund. The total of these costs is known as the expense ratio, which is expressed as a percentage of the fund's average net assets during the year. This annual expense ratio typically ranges

from a low of about 0.2 percent (or $2 per $1,000 in assets) to 2 percent ($20 per $1,000 in assets). Some funds add to their operating expenses a 12b-1 fee, which goes toward paying marketing and distribution costs of the fund. This 12b-1 fee, which is sometimes used instead of a sales load to compensate salespersons, can be as much as 1 percent of assets, or $10 each year for each $1,000 invested.

The average equity fund now charges 1.54 percentage points in expenses, and portfolio transaction costs can bring the total annual expenses to 2 percentage points or more, a levy likely to cut the returns investors earn by 20 percent or more over time. You should favor low-turnover funds. Today's average fund portfolio turnover of 85 percent per year carries transaction costs that reduce returns by as much as one-half to one percentage point over and above the cost of fund expenses (and carries enormous tax costs).

No-Load Funds

No-load funds charge no sales commission because they aren't sold by brokers. You buy no-load funds directly from a mutual fund family or through discount brokerage firms. The debate about load versus no-load continues, with experts divided on which is better. Over the long haul, the two have similar total returns (on the net amount invested after any load). In most instances, the load pays for your broker's time and advice. If you value that, loads may be worth it. You also may pick a load fund because you like its performance or its manager. You also might pay a load to invest in outstanding sector funds.

Many investors need personal assistance and guidance in selecting mutual funds. Others don't. For the many who don't, some 3,000 no-load funds are available to choose from. Assuming the funds are properly selected, no-load funds provide the least costly way to own mutual funds.

You should beware of many apparently no-load funds that have hidden loads. Some have sales charges (12b-1 fees) that are deducted from your returns each year. The total cost may reduce your annual return by an additional one percentage point, with even larger deductions if you redeem your fund shares within five or six years (back-end loads). Other funds use 12b-1 fees, not to pay the salesman, but to promote sales of the fund's shares through aggressive advertising and marketing programs. These fees are paid out of the shareholders' pockets, but provide no net benefit whatsoever to the shareholders. It's not a good deal. So be wary of so-called no-load funds that charge 12b-1 fees. To be called a no-load fund, the National Association of Securities Dealers (www.nasd.com) stipulates that the 12b-1 fee be no greater than 0.25 percent.

How Costs Affect Returns

Operating expenses directly reduce the return that you get from your investment. The impact can be clearly demonstrated. Suppose you put $10,000 into each of two funds, both of which earned an average annual return of 8 percent before taxes. Let's assume that Fund A had a below-average expense ratio of 0.45 percent, and Fund B had annual expenses equal to 1.45 percent (the average expense ratio for a stock fund in 1998). After 20 years, Fund A would have grown to $42,875, whereas Fund B would have grown to $35,569. Thus, a seemingly small difference of 1 percent per year in expenses amounts over 20 years to a difference of $7,306, or more than 70 percent of the initial investment.

Front-end sales charges reduce the amount of money you are putting to work for you in an investment. A $10,000 investment in a fund with a 5 percent load buys $9,500 worth of shares in the fund. It then takes a gain of 5.3 percent merely to get back to even at $10,000. Suppose two funds earn the same average annual return of 7 percent, after expenses, but that Fund A is sold without a load, whereas Fund B imposes a 5 percent load. After 20 years, Fund A would have grown to $38,697, while Fund B would have grown to $36,762. The no-load fund's head start translated into a difference of $1,935, or 19 percent of the original $10,000 investment.

Paying a sales load or higher operating expenses might make sense if the end result were higher returns to the investor. But paying more to purchase shares or to operate a fund doesn't necessarily mean that you receive better portfolio management. According to William Sharpe, recipient of the 1990 Nobel Prize in Economics: "There is virtually no evidence to suggest that funds with higher expense ratios do better, before expenses. Which therefore suggests they will do worse, after expenses."

How to Compare Costs

It's easy to determine the costs of a mutual fund. The Securities and Exchange Commission requires that information about sales charges and operating expenses be disclosed in a document called the *prospectus*, which must be given to all investors at or before the time of purchase. The information about sales charges and expenses is spelled out in a fee table near the front of the prospectus. The table makes it easy to compare the costs of one fund with those of another. Or you can easily access cost and other data on any particular mutual fund at many Internet sites (e.g., www.yahoo.com).

Characteristics of a Successful Mutual Fund

A fund whose shares you are considering to purchase should have the following characteristics:

- *Performance.* This is a mutual fund's reason for being—it should be the driving force behind everything it does, and the fund should pursue it tenaciously.
- *Adherence to its objective.* Every mutual fund has a stated objective and a stated strategy for pursuing that objective. It must have the discipline to stick to all that has been stated in its prospectus. This is important because a mutual fund should be only part of your broad financial plan. For your plan to be successful, all of its parts must perform.
- *Accountability.* Responsibility for a fund's performance rests with the portfolio manager. This accountability is a powerful incentive. The manager should embrace a disciplined, collaborative approach to investing, one in which insights and expertise are shared.
- *Well-managed risk.* There is a difference between risk and risky. Risk is a natural, necessary part of investing. It is the engine that drives reward. Well-managed risk helps you achieve your goals. The best mutual funds identify and manage risk, delivering the right balance of risk and reward.
- *Good communications.* Investing with a mutual fund should be easy and the mutual fund company itself should be easy to work with. Communications should be honest, accurate, and easy to understand.

IN A NUTSHELL

With more than $5.5 trillion entrusted to their care, mutual funds have become the investment of choice for millions of investors. Diversification, professional management, liquidity, and convenience have helped to make mutual funds America's most popular medium for investing.

Why Big Investors Buy Mutual Funds

More and more, substantial investors are using mutual funds to solve at least some of their investment problems. This trend accelerated with the development of money market funds in the 1970s, and today it's no longer unusual for large investors to place multimillion-dollar investments in mutual fund accounts. According to the Investment Company Institute (www.ici.org), institutional investors now account for nearly 50 percent of all mutual fund assets.

Who are these investors and why do they invest in mutual funds? Many of them certainly can afford to hire investment advisers on a private basis. Large shareholders of mutual funds today include wealthy individuals, trustees, pensions, profit-sharing and 401(k) retirement plans, corporate funds, endowment funds, and such institutions as churches, schools, and hospitals. In the last analysis, big investors buy mutual funds for many of the same reasons as small investors.

Performance and Policy

One of the most important reasons major investors choose mutual funds is the availability of past performance records. No other form of investment management can provide prospective clients with so complete and unquestionable a picture of what it has achieved in the past. The investor can easily see how well a particular mutual fund manager has handled the funds under his or her care and if those results are suitable to the investor's own investment needs.

Of value, in addition to an accurate picture of past performance, is a mutual fund's clearly stated position on objectives, policies, and investment holdings. Not only do mutual fund companies have a wide variety of different objectives and policies, they also provide clear descriptions of exactly what these objectives and policies are and how management goes about implementing them.

Convenience, Simplicity, and Liquidity

For all large investors, the convenience of owning shares in one or a few mutual funds is an important benefit. Contrast this with owning individual shares of stock in many companies, collecting dividends on each, and having to keep records of each transaction. Recordkeeping alone is a significant problem that is kept to a minimum by owning mutual funds.

Complete liquidity is another benefit that the large investor appreciates. A portion, or the entire amount, of a mutual fund investment can be liquidated quickly and without any concern about disrupting the market in a particular stock or bond.

Finally, with no-load mutual funds investors can get money into and out of the market at no cost: no commission to buy, no cost to sell (in most cases), and no length of time that the investment must remain in effect. Investors have nearly complete flexibility in the handling of their money. Contrast this with the ownership of individual securities, where an investor must pay a commission to buy and again a commission to sell.

Freedom from Care and Responsibility

Even experienced investors often reach the point where they no longer want the responsibility of managing their own investments. The financial universe has become so large and so complex that it is now virtually impossible for any individual to be competent in all its phases. Other investors simply want the peace of mind that comes from letting someone else do the worrying—managers get paid for it. Many investors have bought a stock that looked attractive, only to watch its price immediately drop five or ten points. The volatility of such a stock in a mutual fund would hardly be noticed and is probably offset by another stock that is rising.

This brings us to diversification. Large and experienced investors have come to understand and appreciate the benefits of being diversified. Not only can an investor enjoy the advantages of diversification provided by one mutual fund, he or she also can diversify further by spreading assets over several different funds. This provides the additional safety of multiple managers, each of whom is governed by his or her own set of investment objectives and policies. Different managers, objectives, and policies provide varying results in different economic and market climates, further reducing the risks in a large (or small) account.

For the investor who chooses unmanaged index funds, diversification comes not only from the many stocks held by an individual fund, but also from investing in funds that reflect different universes. For example, the S&P 500 provides an investment in 500 of the largest U.S. corporations. An investor who wants to be represented in foreign stocks, real estate investment trust companies (REITs), small cap companies, or bonds—to name a few—can find index funds that have those objectives.

Trust Accounts

Mutual fund shares have become increasingly accepted as prudent investments for trust accounts and by the banks and trust companies that manage trust accounts. This has been especially true with the advent of money market funds and with the growing acceptance of common stocks as suitable investments for trusts.

The prudent man rule, set forth in 1830 by Justice Samuel Putnam of the Supreme Judicial Court of Massachusetts in *Harvard College v. Amory,* is a standard that can easily be met by careful selection and investment in mutual funds. As Justice Putnam stated:

> All that can be required of a trustee . . . is that he shall conduct himself faithfully and exercise a sound discretion. He is to observe how men of prudence, discretion, and intelligence manage their own affairs, not in regard to speculation, but in regard to the permanent disposition of their funds, considering the probable income as well as the probable safety of the capital to be invested.

The purchase of mutual fund shares answers the need for careful selection, adequate diversification, and watchfulness that are essential to prudent investing in stocks and bonds. It is a job that requires continuous diligence. Many trustees, small institutions and individuals alike, simply do not have the time, background, or expertise to undertake this effort. Beyond that, many small trusts do not have sufficient assets to provide the diversification that prudence requires.

Retirement Plans and Institutions

For pension, 401(k), and profit-sharing plans, mutual funds offer various advantages. The fiduciary responsibilities implicit in these plans are similar to those faced by the trustees of personal trusts. By using mutual funds, corporate officers maintain control of the plans while meeting the fiduciary requirements of trustees. They can obtain the particular investment objectives and policies that are suitable for their plans while meeting Internal Revenue Service requirements for maintaining the plans' tax-exempt status.

A further advantage of mutual funds for retirement plans is the ease with which mutual fund investments can be evaluated for performance on an annual, or more frequent, basis. This evaluation can be difficult for a plan that is invested in a variety of individual stocks and bonds. It is also simple to determine the value of a withdrawing participant's account and to reallocate any forfeited amounts among remaining participants.

Further simplifying the problems of setting up retirement plans is the availability of prototype pension, 401(k), and profit-sharing plans that have been developed by many mutual fund organizations, making it unnecessary for companies to devote the time and expense of drawing up their own plans. Individual retirement accounts (IRAs) and retirement plans for self-employed individuals also are offered by most mutual fund groups.

Among the largest investors in the shares of mutual funds are schools, colleges, foundations, hospitals, religious organizations, libraries, unions, and fraternal associations. Such institutions often don't have qualified personnel to handle the proper investment of their funds. But even when they do, they often find it more convenient and prudent to invest in mutual funds for the same reasons that other large investors invest in mutual funds—namely, diversification, investment management, and defined investment objectives and policies.

IN A NUTSHELL

Large investors use mutual funds for many of the same reasons as do small investors. By experience, they have found that mutual funds provide the benefits they seek in a more cost-effective and convenient way than would otherwise be possible. Here are some key advantages of mutual funds:

- Past performance is easily evaluated.
- Investment objectives and policies are clearly spelled out.
- A diversified portfolio of investments can be set up quickly and at no cost.
- Accounts can be readily liquidated without disrupting the market.
- Investors are relieved of the responsibility and care of managing their investments.

Indexing: Building an Entire Portfolio with One Fund

Through an investment strategy known as indexing, you can invest in a replication of the whole stock or bond markets, or in specific segments of either market, by buying shares in a single fund. Any investor, even with very limited funds, can invest in a fund that holds all 500 of the largest U.S. companies, a representation of small capitalization (small cap) companies, a representation of the total U.S. stock market, or a representation of foreign stock markets.

A market index measures changes in the stock, bond, and commodities markets, reflecting market prices and the number of shares outstanding for the companies in the index. Well-known market indexes include the S&P 500, the New York Stock Exchange (NYSE) Index, and the Wilshire 5000. Indexing describes the investment approach of attempting to parallel the investment returns of a specific stock or bond market index. An increasing number of individual investors, pension funds, and institutional investors choose indexing.

It has been said that active managers possess special skills that allow them to pick and choose in specialized markets and avoid poor investments. They are also expected to lose less during market downturns because they have the flexibility to raise cash levels or move out of stock markets that show the least favorable prospects. These attributes are considered to be advantages over index funds which, by charter, must be fully invested in a relatively fixed list of stocks at all times.

The theory, however, often doesn't work out in practice. For example, the average emerging markets stock fund produced a negative 26.8 percent return in 1998. Two major index funds, the Dimensional Fund Advisors Emerging Markets Fund and the Vanguard Emerging Markets Fund, lost just 9.4 percent and 18.1 percent, respectively. This poor relative performance of active managers of emerging markets stock funds relative to index funds was accompanied by a similar failure in the U.S. markets. During the steep market decline of the 1998 third quarter, actively managed funds also did worse than index funds.

Because actively managed funds have a hard time beating their index benchmarks, many investors completely ignore managed funds. In fact, you can build your entire portfolio with index funds, an approach that has been catching on with many individual investors; some experts estimate that as many as 25 percent of investors are now "indexing" their portfolios.

How an Index Fund Works

An index fund manager tries to replicate the target index investment results by holding all, or a representative sample, of the securities in the index. Indexing is a passive approach to investing. No attempt is made to use traditional active money management techniques in selecting individual stocks or industry sectors in an effort to outperform the indexes. The result is an investment approach emphasizing broad diversification and low portfolio trading activity.

Studies have shown that the stock market overall has had a long-term average return of about 11 percent per year. But that 11 percent is the gross return (before expenses such as management fees, commissions, and other costs). The net return can be significantly less, resulting in a number well below the market return. Here's how it works: Most mutual funds have such costs as advisory fees, distribution charges, operating expenses, and portfolio transaction costs. According to Lipper Analytical Services, these costs total approximately 2 percent of investor assets on average. Thus, the net average return to investors is 9 percent, not the 11 percent provided by the market averages.

A properly run index fund pays no advisory fees (because there is no active investment management), keeps operating expenses at a very low level, and keeps portfolio transaction costs at the minimum. The lower the expenses a fund incurs, the closer the fund's performance will be to the index it tracks.

The Birth of Index Funds

The first index mutual fund was formed in 1975 by The Vanguard Group (www.vanguard.com). It was modeled on the Standard and Poor's 500-stock index. After a shaky start (mediocre relative returns during its first five years) and minuscule assets (just $90 million in 1980), the fund became a huge success. The Vanguard 500 Index Fund (www.vanguard.com), with assets of $74 billion in early 1999, has produced better 15-year returns—because of its large cap stock bias—than those of the total stock market and is now the second largest fund in America (the largest with its companion 500 Index Institutional Fund).

In the early years, there were lots of jokes about Vanguard's index fund. "Index funds are un-American," "Bogle's folly" (John Bogle, chairman of Vanguard, was the driving force behind Vanguard's index fund), and "seeking mediocrity" were hardly the worst things that were said. But as the performance data were evaluated, it is no longer a competitive joke. Although uncopied—even shunned—for a full decade, Vanguard's index fund has now been joined by some 120 competitive index funds. About one-third of these have reasonable expense ratios (0.25 percent or less), but 20 have too-high ratios of 0.75 percent or more, and 25 even charge sales loads or 12b-1 fees. They don't seem to realize that minimal cost accounts for virtually all of the index advantage.

The indexing concept is much broader than a single index fund, however. First, true indexing works best against the total stock market, and the all-market fund is only at the beginning of its acceptance. Second, for investors who, for one reason or another, seek to earn higher returns in specific broad market sectors, funds modeled on growth indexes and value indexes, as well as small cap and midcap indexes, are now available. Studies have made clear that index funds would have produced highly effective risk-adjusted returns in each. Index funds are in the incipient stage, too, in the bond market and the international market, where they are equally effective.

Indexing is threatening to become the new Holy Grail for fund investors, and it should be. If investors increasingly see the merit of indexing strategies as a means to outpace the long-term returns of individual managed funds—a point that studies abundantly demonstrate—it will become increasingly difficult for sponsors of traditional funds to compete.

FIGURE 28.1 / OWNING THE WHOLE MARKET WITH A SINGLE INDEX FUND

	$10,000 INVESTED FOR 15 YEARS FROM JUNE 1983 TO JUNE 1998	
	ACTIVELY MANAGED STOCK FUND	TOTAL MARKET INDEX STOCK FUND*
Initial cost	$10,000	$10,000
Final value	$66,800	$90,300
Average annual total return	13.5%	15.8%
Percent of market return	84.0%	99.0%

---

*Wilshire 5000

Investing in the Whole Market

During the past 15 years, the record of indexing has been truly remarkable; the total stock market index (the Wilshire 5000 index) has outpaced the average diversified equity fund by 2.3 percentage points per year. The index fund captured 99 percent of the market's annual return of 16 percent. Managed equity funds captured just 84 percent. As shown in Figure 28.1, the added return on a $10,000 investment was $23,500, some two and one-half times the entire value of the initial investment. This 2.3 percent difference arises largely because the total costs of the managed funds averaged about 2 full percentage points. This 15-year equity fund comparison amply justifies a simple index approach to capture the highest realistically possible portion of the markets' returns—slightly less than 100 percent.

By investing in a total stock market index fund (you will own the entire U.S. stock market), making no effort to select the best manager, making no attempt at market timing, keeping transaction activity low, minimizing taxes, and eliminating the excessive costs of investing that characterize most mutual funds, you will have an investment strategy that works. The indexing advantage became even more pronounced in 1998 with an astonishing advantage of 15 percentage points over the average equity fund manager: 22 percent versus 7 percent for the average fund through December 1.

Many investment professionals believe that the S&P 500 should be the universal measuring stick for manager performance. As anyone who has ever considered the issue knows, however, the S&P 500, invested

100 percent in stocks at all times, is a large cap index. Currently representing three-fourths of the market value of all U.S. stocks, it would seem a huge sample—and in the aggregate sense it is—but it completely ignores one-fourth of the market: midcap and small cap stocks, which periodically prove to have quite different performance characteristics. During most of the 1990s (through 1998), large cap stocks carried the day with an annualized return of 17.3 percent, compared with 13.3 percent for the rest of the market (Wilshire 4500 equity index).

Investing in Index Funds

Indexing's main appeal is to long-term investors who seek a very competitive return through broadly diversified portfolios. Index funds provide investors with a high degree of relative predictability in an uncertain stock market. Nothing can ensure absolute returns, but these investors can feel confident that their investment shouldn't be a dramatic underperformer relative to other funds investing in the same types of securities, and over the long term index funds should deliver a very competitive relative performance.

With the increasing selection of indexes to choose from (The Vanguard Group alone has 27 index funds), you now can buy into the whole stock market or into particular segments of the securities markets. Although most of the focus on index investing has been on funds that attempt to replicate the S&P 500, you now can find funds that seek to match other indexes, both in the U.S. market and abroad. Listed below are some of your choices:

- *Dow Jones Industrial Average:* The oldest, best known, and most widely quoted index consists of 30 companies, chosen as representative of the broad market and of American industry.
- *Dow Jones world stock index:* Consists of approximately 2,600 stocks of U.S. and foreign companies that are located in 25 countries. The index has approximately 120 industry groups and subgroups divided into nine broad market sectors.
- *Lehman Brothers aggregate bond index:* Consists of more than 6,000 individual investment-grade, fixed-income securities, including U.S. Treasury and government agency securities, corporate debt obligations, and mortgage-backed securities.
- *Morgan Stanley capital international—select emerging markets free index:* A broadly diversified index consisting of approxi-

mately 460 common stocks of companies located in the countries of 12 emerging markets in Southeast Asia, Latin America, and Europe.

- *Morgan Stanley capital international Europe (free) index:* A diversified index comprising approximately 575 companies located in 13 European countries. This index includes only the shares of companies that U.S. investors are free to purchase.
- *Morgan Stanley capital international pacific index:* A diversified index consisting of approximately 425 companies located in Australia, Japan, Hong Kong, New Zealand, and Singapore. The index is dominated by the Japanese stock market, which represents about 85 percent of its market capitalization.
- *Morgan Stanley REIT index:* Includes the stocks of all publicly traded REITs (real estate investment trusts) that have a total market capitalization of at least $75 million and have enough shares and trading volume to be considered liquid.
- *Russell 2000 small stock index:* A broadly diversified, small capitalization index consisting of approximately 2,000 common stocks. The average market capitalization of stocks in this index is about $250 million.
- *S&P/BARRA growth index:* Consists of stocks selected from the S&P 500 with higher than average ratios of market price to book values.
- *S&P/BARRA value index:* Consists of stocks selected from the S&P 500 with lower than average ratios of market price to book values.
- *Standard & Poor's 500 index:* Measures the total investment return of 500 common stocks, most of which trade on the NYSE and represent about 75 percent of the market value of all U.S. common stocks.
- *Wilshire 4500 index:* Consists of all U.S. stocks that are not in the S&P 500 index and that trade regularly on the NYSE and the AMEX (American Stock Exchange) as well as in the Nasdaq market. More than 5,000 stocks of midsize and small capitalization companies are included in the index.
- *Wilshire 5000 index:* Consists of all regularly and publicly traded U.S. stocks, providing a complete proxy for the U.S. stock market. More than 6,000 stocks—including large, medium, and small cap companies—are included in the index. It represents the value of all NYSE, AMEX, and Nasdaq stocks for which quotes are available.

FIGURE 28.2 / TOTAL RETURN OF THE VANGUARD INDEX 500 FUND, 1981 TO 1998, COMPARED WITH THE S&P 500

YEAR	FUND	S&P 500	YEAR	FUND	S&P 500	YEAR	FUND	S&P 500
1981	− 5.2%	− 4.9%	1987	+ 4.7%	+ 5.1%	1993	+ 9.8%	+10.1%
1982	+20.9	+21.5	1988	+16.2	+16.6	1994	+ 1.1	+ 1.3
1983	+21.3	+22.5	1989	+31.3	+31.7	1995	+37.4	+37.6
1984	+ 6.2	+ 6.3	1990	− 3.4	− 3.1	1996	+22.8	+23.0
1985	+31.2	+31.8	1991	+30.2	+30.5	1997	+33.2	+33.4
1986	+18.0	+18.6	1992	+ 7.4	+ 7.6	1998	ı28.6	+28.8

Investors have wide-ranging interests, and index funds are available for different market sectors. Figure 28.2 shows the total return achieved by the Vanguard Index 500 Fund as well as the return on the S&P 500. The Vanguard fund was chosen for two reasons: (1) It is exceptionally well run, with low costs and a history of consistently coming very close to meeting its stated objective; and (2) it replicates the S&P 500, which has attracted the most attention from investors interested in an index fund investment.

It is only expenses that separate the Vanguard Index 500 Fund from its target, the S&P 500. An index fund's expense ratio (advisory fees, operating expenses, and transaction costs) accounts for most of the difference between the fund's returns and those generated by its target index, so expenses are very important in assessing passively managed (indexed) funds.

Information on Index Funds

As the mutual fund industry continues to spew out new index funds, you might check out the Index Funds Online Web site (www. indexfundsonline.com) for up-to-date information. To help you keep up, this site maintains a list of index funds, a weekly update of performance figures, an indexing library, articles by index fund commentators, and much more. Two recent fund offerings provide examples of different approaches you will find.

In December 1998 the Guinness Flight Wired Index Fund (www. gffunds.com) was introduced to "track the growth of the 40 companies in the Wired index that are building the new economy—not just high-tech companies, but a broad range of enterprises that are using technology, networks, and information to reshape the world," according to *Wired* magazine. The investment strategy of the fund (symbol: GFWIX) is to replicate the performance of the Wired index. In managing the fund, management generally will follow a policy of full replication, meaning the fund generally will invest in all 40 component issues that comprise the Wired index in the proportion they are represented within the index. From time to time management will use a method known as index sampling, an investment technique that seeks to replicate performance of the index by investing in a subset of the 40 component stocks. Some would argue that this strategy doesn't characterize a true index fund because it calls for some degree of management in the portfolio.

The Waterhouse Dow 30 Fund (www.waterhouse.com) is the first no-load, no-transaction-fee index fund that seeks to track the total return of the Dow Jones Industrial Average (the Dow) by investing primarily in the Dow. The minimum initial investment is $1,000 and monthly minimum investments of $100 are available through the firm's Free Periodic Investing Program.

IN A NUTSHELL

You can invest in a replication of the whole stock market, or segments of it, by purchasing shares of a single index fund. Indexing has become the investment strategy of choice among many individual and institutional investors.

Online Mutual Fund Supermarkets

Fund-shopping networks, offered by discount brokers, are among the most convenient services available to mutual fund investors. These networks enable you to diversify your portfolio across a wide range of mutual fund companies by means of one source. When you invest through one of these one-stop services, you can choose from more than 7,400 mutual funds, including 2,200 no-load funds, sponsored by many of America's leading companies and in many cases without paying any transaction fee. And the number continues to grow. According to Morningstar (www.morningstar.com), the networks will become the dominant way to distribute mutual funds.

The basic idea is simple: You can buy and sell shares in numerous mutual funds without paying a transaction fee. You can buy no-load funds for the same cost as going directly to the individual fund companies. And when you select no-load funds, paying no sales commissions or fees, you're putting the full value of your dollars to work in your investments. Transaction fees are charged on certain no-load funds, generally those that have chosen not to participate in the program. In addition, hundreds of load funds also can be purchased in some programs, in which case you'll be charged the sales load as described in the prospectus. Business can be transacted online (or by telephone), and everything is clearly summarized in one statement.

The biggest programs in terms of assets include Charles Schwab's Mutual Fund OneSource, Fidelity's FundsNetwork, Vanguard's Fund-

Access, Waterhouse Securities' Mutual Fund Network, and Muriel Siebert's FundExchange.

How Mutual Fund One-Stop Shopping Works for You

You pay no commissions, loads, or transaction fees to invest in a wide range of no-load funds available from different fund companies. The price you pay is exactly the one you'd pay by investing directly with the fund itself.

Whatever your investment objective, from capital preservation to aggressive growth, a one-source mutual fund service gives you a nearly complete range of funds to choose from to help you reach your objective. You can move easily between funds, even if they are from different fund companies. This way, you can adjust your mutual fund portfolio to reflect changing investment goals or market conditions.

Once you have established an account, you can invest online in hundreds of mutual funds. Some firms offer limited commission-free trading and will permit you to buy funds on margin or sell short, two highly speculative trading techniques.

Because fund companies pay to participate, organizations that offer no-transaction fee mutual fund network services are compensated by fees received directly from the fund companies. These fees range from 0.20 percent to 0.35 percent of the assets managed by the program. As long as these costs are not passed along to shareholders and fund expense ratios stay at reasonable levels, this should not be a problem for investors.

Although the general approaches for companies providing one-stop shopping are straightforward and pretty much the same, some differences do exist. To get started, you must first open a brokerage account with the firm of your choice, which gives you access to the mutual fund network plus the opportunity to trade in stocks, bonds, and other securities. Then, to purchase mutual fund shares, indicate in your online account the name of the fund, the dollar amount you want to invest, and whether you want fund dividends and capital gains paid in cash or automatically reinvested in more fund shares. To sell, you need only specify the fund, the number of shares you wish to sell, and whether you want to receive the proceeds or have them credited to your account.

The fund consolidators (mutual fund one-source brokers) maintain single, multimillion-dollar accounts at the mutual fund families, so they have some flexibility in meeting minimum investment requirements. Schwab's Mutual Fund OneSource program, for instance, has minimums that range from $250 to $2,000, which in some cases is below what you would have to invest when dealing directly with a fund.

One problem with the one-stop shopping system is that several excellent fund families, including T. Rowe Price, USAA, and Vanguard, don't participate in some of the free programs because they don't charge 12b-1 fees, which are used to pay the firms that offer the one-stop services. However, funds from those families are available if a transaction fee is paid. The Vanguard Group, for example, has its own one-stop shopping system under which a fixed service fee is charged for each order (except for Vanguard fund orders, which incur no fee or load). Generally, firms offering the program will let you transfer most outside funds into your consolidated account at no extra cost, making it easy to keep track of your holdings.

The Major Players

Following are some of the major brokerage firms that offer one-stop mutual fund shopping programs.

Fidelity Investments FundsNetwork

www.fidelity.com
800-544-9697

Fidelity FundsNetwork offers access to more than 3,300 Fidelity and third-party mutual funds from over 300 fund companies. Funds-Network offers no-load and load funds with or without transaction fees. More than 800 funds are available without transaction fees.

With your account established, you also can transfer assets from participating fund companies. FundsNetwork offers the convenience of consolidating all your assets in one account, making it easy to trade, exchange, and monitor all of your investments. The minimum investment is $2,500 for nonretirement accounts and $500 for retirement accounts. Some funds may have higher or lower investment minimums and subsequent minimums.

Some fund families require you to pay a transaction fee to Fidelity. For trades placed online via the Web or through Fidelity On-line Xpress, a transaction fee of $28.95 is applied to both buy and sell orders. Higher fees apply for trades placed through a Fidelity representative. You don't pay a transaction fee on load funds, but you're charged a sales load by the fund, a portion of which is paid to Fidelity. Loads are waived on retirement investments in certain Fidelity funds. Investors must pay any fund level expenses, such as asset-based sales charges (12b-1 fees) and other expenses as detailed in the prospectuses.

You receive one consolidated statement showing all activity on all your mutual fund investments—with mutual fund cost-basis reporting to help with your recordkeeping—as well as any other activity in your Fidelity brokerage account. With the Fund Evaluator, you can use Morningstar data to compare and research over 3,000 mutual funds.

Schwab Mutual Fund OneSource

www.schwab.com
800-435-4000

Mutual Fund OneSource offers access to more than 1,000 no-load mutual funds without transaction fees. Transaction fees may apply to certain no-load and low-load funds that don't participate in the Mutual Fund OneSource service. Such funds are subject to Schwab's standard transaction fees in addition to any redemption fees imposed by the fund:

Transaction Size	**Transaction Fee***
$ 1,000 to $14,999	0.7% of principal
$15,000 +	0.7% on the first $15,000
	0.2% on amount over $15,000; capped at $149

*Overriding minimum is $39 per trade for regular trades and $35 per trade for trades placed electronically.

Schwab doesn't charge transaction fees for funds available through its Mutual Fund OneSource or for certain high-load funds. However, if you paid a fee to buy a fund, you will be charged Schwab's normal transaction fee to sell it as well.

All shares of funds purchased through Mutual Fund OneSource and other mutual funds purchased with no transaction fee must be held for more than 180 days from the date of purchase to avoid paying Schwab's short-term redemption fee. The short-term redemption fee is 0.75 percent of principal (or $39, whichever is greater). The maximum fee is $199 for trades placed online.

You can purchase most mutual funds on margin at Schwab. You also can borrow against the mutual funds held in your account. Schwab Funds (Schwab's own funds) cannot be purchased on margin and are not marginable for 30 days from the date of purchase.

Siebert FundExchange

www.msiebert.com
800-872-0666

Siebert FundExchange gives you access to more funds than many of its competitors—more than 7,065 mutual funds, including more than 2,200 no-load funds and more than 1,000 of them with no transaction fees. Funds are offered from more than 325 fund families. In addition to no-load funds with no transaction fees, FundExchange offers many more no-load funds at a flat rate of $35 per transaction, regardless of how much you buy or sell.

FundExchange permits you to hedge against volatility with dollar cost averaging. Through the periodic investment plan, you direct the firm to purchase a fixed dollar amount of a fund at fixed intervals. You can give the order to purchase fund shares on a monthly, quarterly, semiannual, or annual basis.

The minimum initial investment to qualify for no transaction fee is $2,000 for IRA accounts and $5,000 for other personal accounts unless a particular fund specifies a higher amount. To qualify for no-fee redemptions of no-load funds, you must maintain a holding period of three months; otherwise, transaction fees apply.

Vanguard FundAccess

www.vanguard.com
800-992-8327

FundAccess lets you invest in a wide range of non-Vanguard mutual funds, all through the same Vanguard Brokerage Services (VBS) account you use to buy individual stocks, bonds, and options. You can choose from more than 2,000 no-load funds, including more than 800 with no transaction fees.

You can request prospectuses, obtain comprehensive fund information, and use account services at no charge—including cash payment or automatic reinvestment of dividend and capital gains distributions. You receive consolidated quarterly portfolio summaries and account statements that detail your VBS trading activity.

No-transaction-fee funds require a minimum investment of $5,000. Shares held less than one year carry a 1 percent redemption fee. Transaction-fee funds carry a fixed $35 service fee that is assessed per order regardless of share quantity. You can buy, sell, or exchange shares of Vanguard funds through VBS without paying a brokerage fee or load of any kind.

Waterhouse Fund Family Network

www.waterhouse.com
800-934-4443

With an online account you can buy, sell, or exchange more than 7,400 mutual funds, of which more than 1,100 charge no transaction fee. There is no need to complete an application for each mutual fund, no letters to write for redemption, no paperwork. Not all funds within each fund family are available through the no-transaction-fee program. Some funds may charge 12b-1 fees in excess of 0.25 percent.

All of the funds in the no-transaction-fee program are no-loads with the exception of a few (certain funds in the Blanchard and Kaufmann families, for example) that charge 12b-1 fees in excess of 0.25 percent and therefore can't be categorized as no-load funds.

Transaction fees will be reinstated if five or more short-term redemptions of no-transaction-fee funds are executed within a 12-month period. (Short-term redemptions refer to the sale of fund shares held 6 months or less.) Shares purchased prior to a fund being included in the no-transaction-fee program do not qualify for a waiver of the transaction fee on the sale of those shares.

The FundSearch Group at Waterhouse Securities provides independent research and analysis from Morningstar (www.morningstar.com) and Bloomberg Financial Services (www.bloomberg.com) when you are considering a mutual fund or other investment vehicle.

All activity is combined in one consolidated statement, which includes stocks and bonds along with all of your mutual funds. You may borrow against your fund shares to purchase additional shares or for any other purpose. Margin rates are usually below prime.

IN A NUTSHELL

One-stop mutual fund shopping allows you to choose from thousands of funds through one source online, often without paying any fee or commission. All of your mutual fund activity is consolidated in a single statement, offering comprehensive record-keeping and saving time and paperwork in addition to making your tax reporting easier.

The Decreasing Costs of Mutual Funds

Maybe mutual funds don't cost you as much to own as critics have charged. The Investment Company Institute (www.ici.org), the mutual fund trade association, in a recently released study found that the "total shareholder cost" of investing in mutual funds fell more than one third between 1980 and 1997. The study by ICI Chief Economist Brian Reid found that the average cost of investing in a stock fund in 1997 was 1.49 percent of each dollar invested. That was down from 2.25 percent in 1980.

Total shareholder costs represent the costs you incur in purchasing and holding a mutual fund. That includes fund expenses like sales commissions and management fees. Mr. Reid said the decline in costs came because of lower distribution costs; that is, the sum of annual sales loads and 12b-1 fees. They, along with management fees and expenses, account for the costs of owning a mutual fund. Loads were substantially reduced during the period of the study. So were 12b-1 fees, despite their proliferation.

The study was a rebuttal to critics of mutual fund costs, chief among them the SEC. The agency has questioned fixed fund costs in light of the explosive growth in the number of mutual funds and in their assets under management. Today, some $5 trillion is invested in mutual funds, up from just $810 billion ten years ago, according to the ICI. The number of mutual funds has tripled to more than 8,000.

The ICI study drew on a Lipper Analytical Services database of all mutual funds (www.lipperweb.com) and ICI's own data. Those data, however, were sometimes incomplete, so ICI relied on CDA/Wiesenberger (www.wiesenberger.com), Value Line (www.valueline.com), and other sources to fill in some areas. A similar study done by Lipper not surprisingly had similar findings. The Lipper study said the appearance of higher expenses was due largely to the rise in new, high-expense funds; more funds charging 12b-1 fees; and higher service charges.

In an earlier study, the ICI found that 77 percent of investors' accounts were in lower-cost mutual funds. "When properly adjusted (for asset weightings), management fees are actually declining for older, more successful funds," the Lipper study found. Morningstar Director of Research John Rekenthaler said he believes the study's findings are valid, though the study doesn't address the question of how high fees should be in light of the dramatic growth in mutual funds over the period studied, and that costs should have come down a lot more. The other way of looking at it is that most of the mutual fund industry still has some fairly unfriendly practices.

One of the critics who believe mutual fund costs are too high is John C. Bogle, senior chairman and founder of The Vanguard Group (www.vanguard.com). Mr. Bogle avers that costs play a crucial role in shaping long-term fund returns and that a low expense ratio is the single most important reason why a fund does well.

Mutual Fund Charges

The ICI and Lipper studies highlight a part of mutual fund investing that is often overlooked: the various fees involved in the cost of owning a fund. Below are the main ones.

Loads

Loads are the commissions brokers receive for selling mutual funds. They range from 3 percent to 8 percent of your investment. You often have the choice of paying a front-end load when you buy shares or paying a back-end load when you sell. The latter sometimes is offered as a "contingent deferred sales charge" in which the load declines in increments after the fund is held for a specified number of years. Level-load funds charge an annual fee of about 2 percent.

No-load funds charge no sales commission because they aren't sold by brokers. You buy no-load funds directly from the mutual fund family or through discount brokerage firms. The debate about load versus no-load continues, with experts divided on which is better. Over the long haul, the two have similar total returns (on the net amount invested after any load). In most instances, the load pays for your broker's time and advice. If you value that, loads may be worth it. You may also pick a load fund because you like its performance or its manager. You might also pay a load to invest in outstanding sector funds.

Many investors need personal assistance and guidance in selecting mutual funds. Others do not. For the many who don't, there are some 3,000 no-load funds to choose from. Assuming the funds are properly selected, no-load funds provide the least costly way to own mutual funds.

12b-1 Fees

You should beware of many *apparently* no-load funds that charge hidden loads. Some have sales charges (12b-1 fees) that are deducted from your returns each year. The total cost may reduce your annual return by an additional 1 percentage point, with even larger deductions if you redeem your fund shares within five or six years (back-end loads). Other funds use these 12b-1 fees, not to pay the salesperson, but to promote sales of the fund's shares through aggressive advertising and marketing programs. Know that these fees are paid out of the shareholders' pockets, but provide no net benefit whatsoever to the fund's shareholders. So be wary of "no-load" funds that charge noxious 12b-1 fees.

Both load and no-load funds can charge 12b-1 fees. To be called a no-load fund, the National Association of Securities Dealers (www.nasd.com) stipulates that the 12b-1 fee be no greater than 0.25 percent.

Annual Operating Expenses

These cover the ongoing costs of running a fund. They pay for the fund manager, securities trading, account maintenance, printing, postage, and auditing. You may escape loads, but all funds charge annual operating expenses. Management fees account for the largest part of operating expenses, ranging upwards from 0.2 percent.

The average equity fund now charges 1.54 percentage points in expenses, and portfolio transaction costs can bring the total annual expenses to 2 percentage points or more, a levy likely to cut the returns their investors earn by 20 percent or more over time. Favor low-turn-over funds. Today's average fund portfolio turnover of 85 percent per year carries transaction costs that reduce returns by as much as 0.5 to 1 percentage point over and above the cost of fund expenses (and carries enormous tax costs).

IN A NUTSHELL

A low expense ratio is the single most important reason why a fund does well. The surest route to top-quartile returns is bottom-quartile expenses, a fact reaffirmed by all investment equity styles—small-cap or large-cap, growth or value—and all bond fund maturity ranges as well. Lower costs are the handmaiden of higher returns.

A Simple Way to Grow Your Capital and Protect It against Loss

Everyone wants to find a "sure thing," a way to make money without any risk of losing his or her investment. Does it exist? A lot of people say no. They've tried every way they know and still always seem to end up with the short end of the stick. Then there are others who will assure you that they have a surefire investment that can't lose. They're like the penny stock salesperson who calls at home when you're in the middle of dinner and says, "Have I got a deal for you!"

There actually is a simple investment package you can easily put together yourself that will make you money while ensuring a return of your original investment. The only stipulation required to be confident it will work is that you hold on to the investment for the time you originally set up.

The Zero-Coupon Bond Fund/Growth Stock Fund Combination

The concept of this combination investment is easy. You make your investment in two parts: one portion goes into a zero-coupon U.S. government bond fund with a specific target date. The balance goes into a solid growth fund of your choice. You may select any growth fund you believe has potential for capital appreciation in the years ahead. To be sure the plan will work, you must hold the bond (or bond fund) to maturity. At that time you will receive the total of your original combined investment from the zero-coupon fund, plus you will have the value of the growth fund. The growth fund would have to become worthless for you not to make a profit on the investment package. Even then, you will still get back your original investment.

Unlike ordinary U.S. Treasury bonds that pay interest periodically, zero-coupon U.S. Treasury securities (zeros) are issued at deep discount and then redeemed for their full face value at maturity. Investment return comes from the difference between the price at which a zero is purchased and the price at which it matures (or is sold). Because a zero's maturity value is known at the time of purchase, investors have found these securities to be a dependable way to invest for the future.

American Century's Target Maturities Trust (www.americancentury.com) offers a series of mutual funds that seek to track the performance of a direct investment in zero-coupon U.S. Treasury securities. It's important to note that these funds may experience dramatic share price fluctuation in response to changing interest rates, and that shares sold before maturity may produce significant losses or gains.

American Century Target Maturities Trust Funds

Target Date	May 26, 1999 Price per Share	Target Date Value
December 31, 2005	$72.99	$100
December 31, 2010	56.51	100
December 31, 2015	44.72	100
December 31, 2020	32.35	100
December 31, 2025	27.52	100

Let's assume that you have $10,000 to invest and can leave it untouched for a certain number of years. You can set the plan up for any number of years, selecting a fund that will mature on the target date you desire. In this case, assume you want the plan to run for a little less than 21 years and mature on December 31, 2020.

How the Plan Works

1. Invest a portion of your money in a zero-coupon U. S. government bond fund. For instance, in May, 1999, a share of a zero-coupon American Century Target Maturities Trust that matures for $100 in December 2020 could have been purchased for $32.35. To be assured of having $10,000 at that time, you would have bought 100 shares of the fund for a total of $3,235.

The mutual fund shares will mature for a total of $10,000 on December 31, 2020. The U.S. government has always honored its obligations, and you can feel pretty confident that the zero-coupon bond fund shares will be paid as promised at maturity.

2. Invest the balance of the $10,000 in a stock mutual fund with growth potential. For the sake of this example, let's invest it in the Vanguard 500 Index Fund (www.vanguard.com), which is a good representation of the entire stock market. Keep in mind that past performance is not necessarily an indication of future results. However, the history of this fund for the 20-year period ending December 31, 1998, shows that the annual return averaged 18.38 percent per year. If the equity portion of your investment were to produce that kind of return over the 20 years to early 2020, the $7,080 would grow to a value of $179,992 (assuming reinvestment of income and capital gains distributions).

The Payoff

In summary, here is how your investment might look if the next 20 years returned an investment performance that equaled the last 20 years. Obviously, future years may do better or worse than the past.

	Zero-Coupon U.S. Government Bond	S&P 500 Index Fund
Initial Investment	$ 3,235	$ 7,080
Ending Value	10,000	179,992

This is my "sleep-well" investment. No matter what happens to the stock market, your original $10,000 will be safely returned at maturity. Remember, though, that if you need your money early, the zero-coupon government bond fund may be worth more or less than your cost. Due to market conditions even government bonds fluctuate in value prior to maturity.

Tax Considerations

As noted earlier, zero-coupon bonds do not make interest payments to the holder. Instead, they are purchased at a substantial discount and then mature for the face amount of the bond. For tax purposes, however, the holder is considered to receive the interest each year on an imputed basis. Simply stated, you will be taxed annually on the interest even though you don't receive it. For this reason, you may find it advantageous to hold the zero-coupon/equities program in your IRA, 401(k) plan, self-employed retirement plan, or other retirement plan in which taxes are deferred.

IN A NUTSHELL

The zero-coupon bond/growth stock fund combination enables the cautious investor to own a plan that ensures the return of his or her original investment while providing the opportunity for a substantial capital gain. You need only maintain the investment for the time originally stipulated. The idea is particularly attractive in a retirement plan that shields you from taxes until the program has been completed.

Useful Internet Sites
for Investors

AARP Investment Program	www.aarp.scudder.com
Accutrade	www.accutrade.com
ADR.com	www.adr.com
American Association of Individual Investors	www.aaii.com
American Century	www.americancentury.com
American Express Financial Services	www.americanexpress.com/direct
American Stock Exchange	www.amex.com
Ameritrade	www.ameritrade.com
Annual Report Gallery	www.reportgallery.com
Barron's	www.barrons.com
BigCharts	www.bigcharts.com
Bloomberg Financial	www.bloomberg.com
Bonds Online	www.bondsonline.com
Briefing.com	www.briefing.com
Brill's Mutual Funds Interactive	www.fundsinteractive.com
Business Week	www.businessweek.com
CBS MarketWatch	www.marketwatch.com
Chicago Board of Options Exchange	www.cboe.com
CNNfn	www.cnnfn.com
DailyStocks	www.dailystocks.com

Datek Online	www.datek.com
Discover Brokerage	www.discoverbrokerage.com
DLJ Direct	www.dljdirect.com
Dow Jones Markets	www.djmarkets.com
DRIP Central	www.dripcentral.com
Empire Financial Group	www.lowfees.com
E*Trade	www.etrade.com
Excite	www.excite.com
Federal Deposit Insurance Corporation	www.fdic.gov
Federal Trade Commission	www.ftc.gov
Fidelity Investments	www.fidelity.com
Financial Times	www.ft.com
Forrester Research	www.forrester.com
FundFocus	www.fundfocus.com
Fund Spot	www.fundspot.com
Gomez Advisers	www.gomez.com
H&R Block	www.hrblock.com
Hoover's Stock Screener	www.stockscreener.com
IPO Central	www.ipocentral.com
Lombard	www.lombard.com
Marketplayer	www.marketplayer.com
Microsoft MoneyCentral	www.moneycentral.com
Morningstar	www.morningstar.net
National Association of Securities Dealers	www.nasd.com
National Discount Brokers	www.ndb.com
Net Investor	www.netinvestor.com
New York Stock Exchange	www.nyse.com
Online Investor	www.onlineinvestor.com
Philadelphia Stock Exchange	www.phlx.com
Quick & Reilly	www.quickwaynet.com
Quicken	www.quicken.com
Quicken Financial Network	www.qfn.com
Realty Stocks	www.realtystocks.com
Reuters	www.reuters.com
Schwab, Charles	www.schwab.com
Securities and Exchange Commission	www.sec.gov
Securities Industry Association	www.sia.com
Securities Investor Protection Corporation	www.sipc.org
SmartMoney	www.smartmoney.com
Social Security Online	www.ssa.gov
Standard & Poor's Fund Analyst	www.micropal.com

Standard & Poor's Ratings Services	www.ratingsdirect.com
Stock Guide	www.stockguide.com
Stockpoint	www.stockpoint.com
Suretrade	www.suretrade.com
1040.com	www.1040.com
The Motley Fool	www.fool.com
TheStreet.com	www.thestreet.com
T. Rowe Price	www.troweprice.com
TreasuryDirect	www.publicdebt.treas.gov
Vanguard Brokerage Services	www.vanguard.com
Wall Street Access	www.wsaccess.com
Wall Street Journal Interactive Edition	www.wsj.com
Waterhouse Securities	www.waterhouse.com
A. B. Watley	www.abwatley.com
Web Street Securities	www.webstreetsecurities.com
Jack White	www.jackwhiteco.com
Wit Capital	www.witcapital.com
Yahoo! Finance	www.quote.yahoo.com
Zacks Investment Research	www.zacks.com
ZD Interactive Investor	www.zdii.com

G L O S S A R Y

account registration form The form that accompanies a prospectus and is completed by a prospective investor to provide a mutual fund with account name, address, Social Security number, and other pertinent data.

account statement A statement sent by a mutual fund to each shareholder at least annually. It indicates the shareholder's registration, account number, tax ID number, and number of shares owned. It also lists the account activity and gives a summary of dividends and distributions paid during the statement period.

accumulation plan An arrangement whereby an investor makes regular purchases of mutual fund shares in large or small amounts.

adviser See **investment management company.**

all or none A round lot limit that is to be executed in its entirety or not at all.

anticipated growth rate In a zero-coupon bond fund, the anticipated rate at which a share of the fund will grow from the date of purchase to a particular date during the maturity year.

anticipated value at maturity In a zero-coupon bond fund, the anticipated value of the fund's net assets on a particular date during the year of maturity.

asked price The price at which a buyer may purchase shares of a stock or mutual fund. For mutual fund shares, price includes the net asset value per share plus the sales charge, if any.

average cost-double category A category that permits calculation of investment cost by averaging costs of shares held short term with those held long term.

average cost-single category A category that permits calculation of investment cost by averaging the cost of all shares regardless of the holding period.

back-end load A redemption fee charged an investor in certain mutual funds when shares are redeemed within a specified number of years after purchase.

balanced fund A mutual fund that at all times holds bonds and/or preferred stocks in varying ratios to common stocks to maintain relatively greater stability of both capital and income.

bank draft plan A periodic cash investment made through a shareholder's checking account via bank drafts for the purpose of regular share accumulation.

bid price For common stock and closed-end fund shares, the highest price offered at the moment for stock in the public market and the price at which the holder of open-end mutual fund shares may redeem those shares. In most cases, the bid price is the net asset value per share.

blue chip The common stock of large, well-known companies with relatively stable records of earnings and dividend payments over many years.

blue-sky laws Laws of various states regulating the sale of securities, including mutual fund shares, and the activities of brokers and dealers.

bond A security representing debt; a loan from the bondholder to the corporation.

broker A person in the business of effecting security purchase and sale transactions for the accounts of others.

business day A day when the New York Stock Exchange is open for business.

buying a dividend Purchasing shares of a mutual fund just in time to receive the current income or capital gains distribution, a practice that results in an investor receiving a portion of the investment back as a taxable distribution.

cancellation An order that cancels a previously transmitted order (in its entirety) with or without a replacement order. If the original order is executed before a cancel order reaches the floor, you are bound to the original trade.

capital (1) The assets of a business, including plant and equipment, inventories, cash, and receivables; (2) the financial assets of an investor.

capital gains Profits realized from the sale of securities.

capital gains distribution A distribution to shareholders from net capital gains realized by a mutual fund on the sale of portfolio securities.

capital growth An increase in the market value of securities.

cash equivalent A term that refers to, among others, short-term U.S. government securities, short-term commercial paper, and short-term municipal and corporate bonds and notes as well as money market mutual funds.

certificates of deposit (CDs) Interest-bearing certificates issued by banks or savings and loan associations against funds deposited in the issuing institutions.

change Information that alters an existing order. In effect, a change cancels a previously transmitted order and replaces it with new information (e.g., price, shares, limit, etc.).

check-writing privilege A service offered by some mutual funds (particularly money market and bond funds) permitting shareholders of such funds to write checks against their fund holdings.

closed-end fund The mutual fund of an investment company with a relatively fixed amount of capital whose shares are traded on a securities exchange or in the over-the-counter market.

closing price order An order that will be executed during the first session of off-hours trading if there is a matching order to complete the trade. This order is good for the first session only and will expire at the end of the trading session if it is not executed. A closing price order can only be entered during an off-hours trading session.

commercial paper Short-term, unsecured promissory notes issued by corporations to finance short-term credit needs. The maturity at the time of issuance normally does not exceed nine months.

common stock A security representing ownership of a corporation's assets. Meeting the requirements of bonds and preferred stocks takes precedence over the right to common stock dividends.

convertible securities Securities carrying the right to be exchanged for other securities of the issuer (under certain conditions). The term normally applies to preferred stock or bonds carrying the right to exchange for given amounts of common stock.

custodian The bank or trust company that holds all cash and securities owned by a mutual fund. It also may act as transfer agent and dividend disbursing agent.

day order An order to buy or sell that, if not executed, expires at the end of the trading day in which it is entered. All orders are considered day orders unless specified otherwise. All market orders are day orders.

dealer A person or firm who buys and sells securities to others as a regular part of its business.

debenture A bond secured only by the general credit of the corporation.

defensive stock A stock that is expected to hold up relatively well in declining markets because of the nature of the business represented.

defined asset fund A unit investment trust that is a professionally selected portfolio of a fixed number of securities. The trust expires on a specific date.

direct purchase fund A mutual fund whose shares are purchased by an investor directly from the fund at a low charge or no charge.

discount The percentage below net asset value at which the shares of a closed-end fund sell.

distributions Dividends paid by mutual funds from net investment income and payments made from realized capital gains.

diversification Investment in a number of different security issues for the purpose of spreading and reducing the risks that are inherent in all investing.

dividend A payment from income on a share of common or preferred stock.

dollar cost averaging A method of automatic capital accumulation that provides for regular purchases of equal dollar amounts of securities and results in an average cost per share lower than the average price at which purchases have been made.

do not reduce (DNR) A designation used with a limit order to buy, a stop order to sell, or a stop limit to sell that is not to be reduced by the amount of an ordinary cash dividend on the ex-dividend date. DNRs do not apply to other distributions, such as a stock dividend declared by a company.

earnings In respect to common stock, a company's net income after all charges (including preferred dividend requirements) are divided by the number of common shares outstanding.

equity securities The securities in a corporation that represent ownership of the company's assets (generally common stocks).

exchange privilege The right to exchange the shares of one open-end mutual fund for those of another within the same fund group at a nominal charge (or no charge) or at a reduced sales charge.

expense ratio The proportion of annual expenses, including all costs of operation, to average net assets for the year.

fill or kill A market or limited price order that is to be executed in its entirety as soon as it is represented in the trading crowd; if not executed, the order is to be canceled. "Fill or kill" should not be confused with "all or none."

fixed-income security A preferred stock or debt instrument with a stated percentage or dollar income return.

front-end load A sales fee charged investors in certain mutual funds at the time shares are purchased.

general obligation bonds Bonds that are backed by the full taxing power of a state or municipality.

good-till-canceled (GTC) Also known as an open order, it is a limit order to buy or sell that remains in effect until it is either executed or canceled. A GTC order only can be entered or changed during a regular trading session, not in off-hours trading sessions.

good-till-canceled (GTX) Also known as an open order, it is a limit order to buy or sell that remains in effect until it is either executed or canceled. GTX orders participate in after-hours as well as regular trading sessions. More complicated orders are not permitted on a GTX basis and only can be entered during regular trading hours.

government agency issues Debt securities issued by government-sponsored enterprises, federal agencies, and international institutions. Such securities are not direct obligations of the Treasury but involve government guarantees or sponsorship.

growth stock A stock that has shown better-than-average growth in earnings and is expected to continue to do so as a result of additional resources, new products, or expanded markets.

hedge A security transaction that reduces the risk on an already existing investment position.

hedge fund A mutual fund that hedges its market commitments by holding securities it believes are likely to increase in value and at the same time sells short other securities it believes are likely to decrease in value. The only objective is capital appreciation.

income The total amount of dividends and interest received from a fund's investments before deduction of any expenses.

income fund A mutual fund whose primary objective is current income.

individual retirement account (IRA) A tax-saving retirement program for individuals established under the Employee Retirement Security Act of 1974.

inflation Persistent upward movement in the general price level of goods and services that results in a decline in the purchasing power of money.

investment adviser See **investment management company.**

investment company A corporation or trust (or mutual fund) through which investors pool their money to obtain supervision and diversification of their investments

Investment Company Act of 1940 A federal statute enacted by Congress in 1940 for the registration and regulation of investment companies by the Securities and Exchange Commission.

investment management company An organization employed by a mutual fund to give professional advice on the fund's investments and asset management practices (also called *adviser*).

investment objective The goal of an investor or investment company that may be growth of capital and income, current income, relative stability of capital, or some combination of these aims.

investment policies The means or management techniques that an investment manager employs in an attempt to achieve the stated investment objective.

investment trust See **investment company.**

Keogh plan A tax-favored retirement program for self-employed persons and their employees.

leverage For an individual investor or mutual fund, the effect of using borrowed money to magnify changes in assets and earnings.

limit order An order to buy or sell a stated amount of a security at a specified price—or at a better price if obtainable.

liquid assets Assets that are easily converted into cash or exchanged for other assets.

liquidity A characteristic of assets that can be easily converted into cash or exchanged for other assets.

load See **sales charge.**

long An investor's net ownership position in a particular security.

low load An indication that the load (sales fee) charged to investors in certain mutual funds is no greater than 3 percent of the amount invested.

management company See **investment management company.**

management fee The charge made to an investment company for supervising its portfolio. It frequently includes various other services and is usually a fixed or reducing percentage of average assets at market value.

management record A statistical measure, expressed as an index, of what an investment company management has accomplished with the funds at its disposal.

market order An order to buy or sell a stated amount of a security at the best price obtainable at the time during the normal trading session that the order reaches the trading floor.

money market fund A mutual fund whose investments are in short-term debt securities and is designed to maximize current income with liquidity and capital preservation.

municipal bond fund A mutual fund that invests in diversified holdings of tax-exempt securities, the income from which is exempt from federal taxes.

mutual fund See **open-end investment company.**

National Association of Securities Dealers (NASD) An organization of brokers and dealers in the over-the-counter securities market that administers rules of fair practice and rules to prevent fraudulent acts for the protection of the investing public.

net asset value (NAV) NAV per share equals the total assets of a mutual fund at market value less current liabilities and divided by the number of shares outstanding.

no-load fund A mutual fund selling its shares at net asset value without any sales charges.

odd lot A unit of trading that is less than the normal trading lot (i.e., a round lot). In stock trading, any purchase or sale of fewer than 100 shares is considered an odd lot, although inactive stocks generally trade in round lots of 10 shares. An investor buying or selling an odd lot may pay a higher rate than someone making a round lot trade. This odd lot differential is usually one-eighth of a point ($.125) per share, but may be higher depending on the security.

offering price See **asked price.**

open-end investment company An investment company whose shares are redeemable at any time at its approximate net asset value.

open order See **good-till-canceled (GTC)** and **good-till-canceled (GTX).**

option A right to buy or sell specific securities at a specified price within a specified period.

performance See **management record.**

performance fund An investment company that appears to emphasize short-term results and usually has had rapid turnover of portfolio holdings. It also may refer to any fund that has had an outstanding record of capital growth.

portfolio The securities owned by an investor or an investment company.

portfolio turnover The dollar value of purchases and sales of portfolio securities, not including transactions in U.S. government obligations and commercial paper.

preferred stock An equity security, generally carrying a fixed dividend, whose claim to earnings and assets must be paid before common stock is entitled to share.

premium The percentage above net asset value at which the shares of a closed-end fund trade.

private placement The sale of an issue of debt or equity securities to a single buyer or to a limited number of buyers without a public offering.

prospectus The official document that describes the shares of a new issue. This document must be provided to each purchaser under provisions of the Securities Act of 1933.

proxy Written authority to act or speak for another party. Proxies are sent to shareholders by corporate management to solicit the authority to vote the shareholders' shares at annual meetings.

real estate investment trust (REIT) A company that owns and manages a portfolio of real estate properties, mortgages, or both.

redemption price See **bid price.**

registered investment company An investment company that has filed a registration statement with the Securities and Exchange Commission under the requirements of the Investment Company Act of 1940.

registration statement The document containing full and accurate information that must be filed with the Securities and Exchange Commission before new securities can be sold to the public.

regulated investment company An investment company that has elected to qualify for the special tax treatment provided by Subchapter M of the Internal Revenue Code.

reinvestment privilege A service offered by most mutual funds and some closed-end funds through which dividends from investment income may be automatically invested in additional full and fractional shares.

round lot The generally accepted unit of trading on a securities exchange. On the New York Stock Exchange, for example, a round lot is 100 shares for stock and $1,000 or $5,000 for bonds. For some inactive stocks, the round lot is 10 shares.

sales charge An amount that, when added to the net asset value of mutual fund shares, determines the offering price. It covers commissions and other costs and is generally stated as a percentage of the offering price.

sales commission See **sales charge.**

secondary distribution The sale of a large block of existing, not newly issued, securities with the proceeds going to the present holders rather than to the issuing firm.

secondary offering See **secondary distribution.**

Securities and Exchange Commission (SEC) An independent agency of the U.S. government that administers the various federal securities laws.

short A security position in which the security has been borrowed and sold but not yet replaced.

simplified employee pension (SEP) plan A retirement plan whereby employers can make deductible contributions to individual retirement accounts (IRAs) established for their employees.

specialty or specialized fund An investment company concentrating its holdings in specific industry groups.

spread The difference between the bid and asked prices for a particular security. A large spread often indicates inactive trading of the security.

statement of additional information A statement that contains more complete information than is found in a prospectus and that is on file with the Securities and Exchange Commission.

stop-limit order An order to buy or sell at a specified price (limit price). Once an order trades at the stop price, the order becomes a limit order, not a market order; it is a combination of a stop order and a limit order.

stop order An order to buy or sell at the market price once the security has traded at a specified price called the *stop price*. A stop order to buy, always at a price above the current market, is usually designed to protect a profit or to limit a loss on a short sale. A stop order to sell, always at a price below the current market, is usually designed to protect a profit or to limit a loss on a security already purchased.

total return A statistical measure of performance reflecting the reinvestment of both capital gains and income dividends.

turnover ratio The extent to which an investment company's portfolio (exclusive of U.S. government obligations and commercial paper) is turned over during the course of a year.

12b-1 fee The fee charged by some funds, permitted under a 1980 Securities and Exchange Commission rule (for which it is named), to pay for distribution costs such as advertising or broker commissions. The maximum that may be charged is 1 percent of a fund's net asset value.

unit investment trust A portfolio made up of a fixed number of professionally selected securities. The trust expires on a specific date.

unrealized appreciation or depreciation The amount by which the market value of a portfolio's holdings exceeds or falls short of its cost.

U.S. government securities Various types of marketable securities issued by the U.S. Treasury and consisting of bills, notes, and bonds.

volatility The relative rate at which shares of a security or fund tend to move up or down in price as compared with a particular market index.

withdrawal plan An arrangement provided by many mutual funds by which an investor can receive periodic payments in a designated amount, which may be more or less than the actual investment income.

yield Income received from investments, usually expressed as a percentage of the market price.

yield to maturity The rate of return on a debt security held to maturity. Both interest payments and the capital gain or loss are taken into account.

INDEX